TESTIMONIALS

"The information in this book will give you all the tools you need to know to incorporate a successful business model of YOU! You will become your own Chief Life Officer, in charge of better relationships, communications and goal setting. This book gives you the keys to unlock and understand yourself in relation to family, friends and co-workers."
Beth Henry, President, Generation Works

"After reading Chief Life Officer, by Amy Remmele, I immediately saw how this book would relate to my own life. As a business owner for the past 25 years, I am forever struggling between my work life and personal life....going back and forth between the two with no real satisfaction. This book taught me the importance of setting goals, understanding how critical open communication is and how to cultivate relationships. More importantly, Chief Life Officer helped me clarify the direction I need to take in both my personal and professional life. Lyrics from The Plain White Rapper, which preceded each chapter, added a unique and interesting depth giving me a preview of what I would be reading about next, truly a clever touch! I look forward to applying the lessons learned in Amy's book to my own Me, Inc!"
Joyce S. DeLong, Owner, Insty-Prints Business Printing Services

"Amy Remmele has a provocative self-help challenge for us all...to organize, analyze, invest in and develop ourselves just like a successful business. Give yourself a promotion and become the Chief Learning Officer of Me, Inc!"
Brian Walter, Communications Consultant, Owner,
Extreme Meetings, Inc.

"Any businessperson, and, in fact, any person will learn great lessons about how to more effectively operate their organization or life thanks to Amy Remmele's insightful Chief Life Officer. Every nugget motivated me to contemplate my personal, as well as my professional life. And, I did not have to do any overt psychoanalysis to get it. I am a business person, specifically a marketer, and the language that I relate to everyday is perfectly relevant to both sides of my being. I am a product, no different from the products marketed by Microsoft or Proctor & Gamble. A successful household can operate under the same basic premise as a growing multinational corporation, and thanks to Amy (with help from the Plain White Rapper) I can use the same terminology when I talk about either."
Marc Adler, Partner, Flynn & Friends

"Amy and I have worked together for over ten years. I know from personal experience that she lives what she teaches. The principles in Chief Life Officer are tried and true with Amy's individual clients and with her business clients. Chief Life Officer is so comprehensive that I will use the concepts in my personal life and in my life as a Sales Professional."
Cindy Karl, Senior Executive Multi Media Consultant,
White Directory Publishers

"It is not often that by the end of the first chapter of a book you can feel your own perspective change. Chief Life Officer does just that, breaking down the complex theories and practices involving every relationship in life, into simple, easy to follow, and easy to visualize business terms that most of us use every day. Anyone who lives a hectic life can take something away from reading this book."
Steve Cichon, WBEN Radio News Anchor/Reporter

"Finally an author that practices what she preaches. Amy Remmele lives what she writes about every day. A down-to-earth, layman's version of how to be successful. Many of us are already doing these things, but not in as useful or as productive a way. Couldn't have come out at a better time."
Joe Chille, Operations Manager, Regent Broadcasting Buffalo

Chief

Life

Officer

Amy Remmele

New York

Chief Life Officer
Your Life is the Most Important Business You'll Ever Own

Paperback ISBN 978-1-60037-593-4

Hardcover ISBN 978-1-60037-594-1

Library of Congress Control Number: 2009921616

MORGAN · JAMES
THE ENTREPRENEURIAL PUBLISHER

Morgan James Publishing, LLC
1225 Franklin Ave., STE 325
Garden City, NY 11530-1693
Toll Free 800-485-4943
www.MorganJamesPublishing.com

In an effort to support local communities, raise awareness and funds, Morgan James Publishing donates one percent of all book sales for the life of each book to Habitat for Humanity. Get involved today, visit **www.HelpHabitatForHumanity.org.**

Chief Life Officer is dedicated to the co-owners of the best We, Inc in the universe – my husband, Kent, and my three children, Chelsea, Devon and Holden. They *are* my CEO Roundtable.

Table of Contents

Chapter 1

Your Life Is the Most Important Business You Will Ever Own: An Introduction To *Chief Life Officer (CLO)*

While my background is in psychology and mental health and I have spent years working with individual clients, I have always been fascinated by sales, marketing and business management. Of course, when I decided to take psychology into businesses, I needed to go back to "school" to learn the lingo and concepts the members of my new clientele were using. I soaked up this education and it soon became second nature to think of my individual and family clients as individual and co-owned businesses. I found that the analogies I was using to illustrate points to them, and the direct advice and guidance I was giving, were routinely involving solid, tested business models, and that I was striving to help them go from *Good to Great*, as the title of that wonderful business book by Jim Collins puts it. My clients resonated remarkably to these metaphors and they made faster and better progress using them than they had made when I was sticking strictly to clinical concepts or every-day language. The clinical concepts needed to be explained before they could be used, and they were sometimes just too convoluted to be useful at all. The shortcoming in using everyday language was that this language was the one my clients were already using, and they were coming to me because that common style of thinking and speaking was not getting them unstuck from their sticking points.

Having such a comfortable, usable language is critical. Most of us just know "snow," perhaps with subtypes of "wet/heavy" and "light/feathery." Skiers know "powder," "deep powder" "granular," "hard-packed" and so on. Eskimos identify dozens of types. Are there really more or different forms of snow at a ski resort or in Alaska than there are in our driveways? I doubt it. But Eskimos and skiers find it useful to name varieties of snow most of us care nothing about because *it makes a difference to them.* So our language is shaped by the environment in which we live and by the stuff we do in that environment. But the ways we see the environment, *including people,* and the ways we experience and interact with the environment and people, are in turn shaped by the language and concepts we apply to them. If I say, "You have a fear of heights," I will probably treat you more kindly and interact with you more gently than if I call you "chicken." And our relationship will probably be even nicer if we share a little joke about your being "elevation-challenged." We know that it makes a difference to call people "developmentally disabled" instead of "mentally retarded," a "sanitation engineer" is not the same as a "garbage man," and so forth.

As a way to get a firmer understanding and grip on this physical world in which we live, I have found myself feeling very much at home with business language and ideas. It fits the environment I live in, the twenty-first century capitalist free world. Thinking and speaking in terms of business has in turn *usefully* shaped the ways I perceive people and their interactions with each other. It has helped me to "see what is really going on" when dealing with people as individuals, couples or families and as members of business or professional organizations and practices. And when I combined the business ideas with my store of psychological knowledge, it was a powerhouse, and it created the basis for this book.

There is a guiding metaphor to *CLO.* It portrays life, and urges you to think of *your* life, as a business. No, it does not have to be nothing but a business. Life is also love and hassles, glorious highs and dismal lows, transcendent moments that are sublime and grounding moments that remind you how earthbound you really are. But then again, for a business to succeed, someone has to love it, and yet it will always present difficulties. The general business cycle, and your business, too, will certainly have its high-flying times and tumbling-down times. Clinching the big deal will be fantastic, and then meeting with your accountant will ground you with a black-and-white reality check. Business is life itself, and life is very business-like.

All business-based concepts in *CLO* will be explained and illustrated with examples. There will be psychology, since we are first and foremost living, behaving creatures. There will be some theory but mostly practical, immediately usable concepts. And you will find that the interweaving of business and psychology will make the metaphor and analogy of your life as a business come alive.

I want to take a moment to explain how I begin the chapters of *CLO*. Each chapter begins with a rap that gives a brief overview of what is to come. One of the characters that I morph into during my seminars is "The Plain White Rapper." She has a unique way of spinning the material that is being covered and she breaks the ice in an unusual and spirited way. Many people resonate to her style. I talk with audiences about how we deal with fun and exciting events and opportunities by teaching that they need to be done in a state of "grace," tempered with safety and caution. We spend a great deal of time reining ourselves and our children in during fun times. These reins and the idea of "grace" are what keep us from going out of control. Roller coasters, for example, may feel out of control and they create great excitement, but they must meet standards of safety and we wait our turn in a line and follow strict rules in order to enjoy this type of fun. These factors are the state of grace surrounding roller coasters. The flip side of the fun and excitement coin, the serious conflicts and decisions that are necessary to manage a successful life, must also be done in a state of grace. Adding some fun and unique twists to these times causes more of our brain to engage and invites more parts of our whole self into the process. So consider The Plain White Rapper my way of surrounding a serious topic with a state of grace. Feel free to read the raps using your own rhythm, or go to the bonus page in the back of this book and download the audio to hear The Plain White Rapper perform the chapter raps. Here is one now!

Here's your introduction to this wonderful book,
After which you'll really want to take a deeper look.
You might be in the habit of skipping introductions,
But you'll want to stay with this one for your reading instructions.

To get your attention, chapters open with a rap,
Then a writing style is added to make your fingers snap.
The content's sometimes easy, but at times you're gonna wrestle
Getting this material into your thinking vessel.

But I assume you are smart and a serious kind,
So all you really need to bring is an open mind.
Morgan James agreed to publish this because it is unique,
So dive right in and start to get your very first peek.

The Plain White Rapper

As the rap says, bring an open mind to your reading of *CLO*. First, be willing to entertain the possibilities I suggest, and leave any preconceived notions behind. For years, my husband, as a psychologist in private practice, vehemently rejected the idea that he was a businessman, believing only that he was a clinician, a provider of service. He thought that it would somehow diminish him to be involved in "business." But his life is now better, and his prosperity more, since he has realized that unless he tends to the *business* of his practice, he will not be there to act as a clinician and service provider. And even from the standpoint of his own psychology, now that he is honest about being a business owner, he can be much more focused in the therapy room.

So the first form of open-mindedness I ask you to bring to reading *CLO* is receptivity, being open to how it applies to you. The second form is in the reverse direction, openness to how you can apply yourself to the ideas in *CLO*. Lessons learned by reading alone are the most shallowly learned and least retained. Lessons learned and then experimented with, tried out, and adapted for use in life, are vastly better learned and retained than those taken in by passive reading only. Lessons learned *and then taught to others* are the best learned and retained, so pass on what you learn. Make your life a laboratory where you experiment with the new ideas. Take the tools and behavioral suggestions I give you out for test drives. That way, some or many of them are bound to become integral parts of the way you think, perceive and act.

CLO is written for

- People who are starting up their own new life business, a "Me, Inc." This group will be mainly young people, especially college students or bright high school graduates, who want to start their adult lives on a sound psycho-educational/ business-minded basis.

- People who are revamping and restarting their Me, Inc. These will be people who may have come to see that their earlier lives had been misguided or not "true to themselves." They may, for example, be survivors of a bad or "poor fit" marriage, people recovering from addictions, or people who for a time lived their lives by the wrong lessons learned in dysfunctional families.

- People who are starting up a partnership, a "We, Inc." In this group are the recently married, those who are considering marriage, couples starting a family, and business partners in a new venture.

- People having troubles in their We, Inc relationships. These include married couples or those involved in other long-term, serious relationships who are experiencing poor communication, excessively frequent conflict, or unresolved issues in particular areas such as money, intimacy, child-raising or lifestyle choices. They also include people having problems with one or more members of their families of origin (the folks who installed those buttons that get pushed so often). Finally, business partners who are at odds are also candidates to benefit from this book.

- People who for any reason are curious about human nature, how it works, and how it applies to them. This group can contain those who simply want to add another thoughtful, well-written book with a unique twist to the list of self-improvement volumes they have already digested.

So, let's get started. Your Me, Inc is waiting for you.

Chapter 2

Only Sell What You Produce:
The Departments of Me, Inc

Every business has departments whether large or small,
So you better know who's who and stay on the ball.
At the start, Me Inc will need a mission and a vision,
And if these aren't on target there will be a collision.

Know your company's heart and deep down soul,
Otherwise there'll be a fall and a terrible toll.
R and D brainstorms ideas and invents,
At the company meeting they will present.

Production will now take it down the line from here.
There will be obstacles around which to steer.
They take the ideas and mold them into real,
Hoping that the budget is on an even keel.

If all is good, we move to the Marketing department,
The idea will no more be in a secret compartment.
Marketing and sales will be bragging up and down,
And smiling 'cause they know Me is the word around town.

But now we need departments for all the self parts.
It's okay to keep moving cuz we have the smarts.
Who would have thought we needed Customer Service?
It will be okay, though, just don't get nervous.

HR watches out for the people and the rules.
They have to stay objective, they can't be fools.
And even in a perfect world, things get broken,
So save some space for the room of the unspoken.

The product is great, but we'll do good repairs,
Always sure our customers don't have despairs.
As we move along smooth it's time to get in sync.
And the on-your-own Me may become We, Inc.

The Plain White Rapper

Every business has departments. In large businesses, there are numerous, obvious departments. Each of them usually has several employees and a manager. This department manager reports to a manager higher up in the company until everyone is reporting to the "top dog." And in very large companies, of course, even the top dog has to report to boards and to stockholders. In a small business, one person may be all of the departments, but there are still departments. For our purposes, let us consider that you as an individual are a small business, a Me, Inc. But if you have a family, then your family is also a business, a We, Inc. As an individual you are responsible in many ways to this larger entity and must report to the co-owners.

The actual number of departments that you have will depend on how complicated your life is and on how many relationships you are involved in. I will take a look here though at some of the universal departments that we all must supervise and maintain.

Production – Getting Down To Your Business

The production departments of a business are the departments that make the products and keep the company running. These are the departments that determine quality and capacity of products. How these departments are run will determine what products actually go up for sale, the speed at which they are produced, the waste or prevention of waste that goes into making the products, whether they are good sound products or shabby cheap products, and how secure the company can be in standing behind their products. Your Production Department is (or your production departments are, if you are quite complex and multifaceted) the "real you," what you are capable of producing, how you do under stress, how much you can tolerate. It consists of your deepest, true beliefs, convictions and ideals, your values and your talents. It is what you live with, what you *are* deep down every minute. It is basically what people get when they "buy your product" or enter into a relationship with you.

Your company owns the patent on a very unique product. And while it seems as though everyone can see the product and how it works, the owner of the company is the only person who knows all of the secrets and mechanisms of the product. The owner is the only person who has the blueprints and all of the original "paperwork" on this product. They are locked away in a safe, the contents of which nobody else will ever see.

Before a product is placed on the market, there is some information that the owner must have available, some questions that must be answered. For example, what is unique about this product? What makes this product attractive and desirable? Why would people want this product? Is the product just a nice idea that should have stayed on paper? Or did we go the extra mile, do our research, expand our horizons and put everything into its design? Do we love our product and spend energy and passion developing it?

It is important to answer these questions about your "product" and to be honest with yourself when answering. Take out a sheet of paper and make sure that there are no "industrial spies" from other companies around before you begin.

The 4-1-1 on Me, Inc – The Information Your Company Needs

Write down your beliefs and values. Are you a Capitalist or a Communist? Do you have a strong work ethic or do you think we should all have a "free ride?" Do you like children? Do you want pets? Do you believe in "til death do us part" for marriage? Are you an Isolationist or do you love the new world with its global thinking? Do you believe that parents should be very strict? Will you be taking care of your parents as they age? There are hundreds of items for this list. If you cannot answer them all at once, take your paper with you and write throughout the day or days. When you hear something on the news or when you engage in conversation, stop and take note of what your beliefs and thoughts are about the subject at hand. Write down what your thoughts about the subject tell you about your deeper values and beliefs. In fact, writing "artificial letters," letters that will never be sent, is an excellent way to articulate your beliefs to yourself and to then articulate them to the people in your life. The core beliefs and attitudes that you discover and re-discover through this process are the foundations of your relationships. These are what keep people together and/or drive them apart. The old adage of "birds of a feather flock together" is true. We tend to "hang with" others who share our beliefs and who are in similar circumstances.

When you are happy with the list, start another one. This list is your characteristics or what I refer to as your "I am" list. Each of these items is "I am" followed by one adjective or a short phrase. The "I am" list is *only* your positive qualities. The "I am" format encourages you to think of these as permanent, broadly pervasive qualities which abide within you enduringly. Examples of these are: I am optimistic, I am a fabulous cook, I am peppy, I am caring about my health, I am careful in my business dealings, I am enthusiastic, I am a good listener, I am sensitive, I am attractive, I am proactive, I am balanced between caution and risk-taking, I am a generous friend, I am creative. If you get stuck on this list, ask some of your closest friends and family to help. When you feel satisfied that this list is complete, then you go on to the "negatives" with an "I do/I have" list. Be very careful not to be overly harsh or critical of yourself with this list. You can get help with this list also. The "I do/I have" format encourages you to think of your "negatives" as discrete behaviors or behavioral patterns which can be corrected, as bad actions waiting to be converted to good. Some examples are: I have a short temper, I interrupt when others are talking, I behave lazily at times, I react with defensiveness when I receive criticism, I don't return phone calls soon enough.

Optimists, those people who have more success, better relationships and better health than pessimists, think the way of the "I am" list for positives and the "I do/I have" list for negatives. Optimists see their good qualities as permanent, broad and broadly applicable traits *and* when good things happen to optimists, they assign the cause to these permanent, pervasive qualities. "I got the job as manager because I am great with people and I am persistent." Optimists see their shortcomings as specific behaviors or patterns of behavior which can be corrected or contained. Optimists do not deny they have problems that need to be fixed, but they describe those problems in ways that suggest they are fixable.

There is also value in knowing your true strengths. Not just those "things" at which you are proficient, but those activities from which you could make a living. Before you list any of these, understand the definition of a real strength, as developed by Marcus Buckingham and Donald Clifton in their book, *Now, Discover Your Strengths*. First, in order for a characteristic to be one of your true strengths, you must have a natural talent in this area. Look around, these are usually easy to recognize. Who looks like they were born doing what they are doing? Who makes it look easy? A musician who can read difficult music almost perfectly the first time he encounters it, an accountant who picks out an error on a spreadsheet in 2 minutes, a dancer who lives the music or a writer whose words just flow, the auto mechanic who knows exactly what causes that awful sound your car is making, the attorney who understands exactly how someone's civil liberties were violated even when the whole world is calling for a public execution, and the physician who diagnoses those odd symptoms that have evaded others, all have a natural talent. If you have a difficult time believing in the need for a natural talent, imagine "products" made without talent. Could just anyone run the four minute mile, even if they trained? Could just anyone golf like Tiger Woods? Could the average person spin a deal like Bill Gates? Could any forensic specialist have written the books behind the CSI television series? No. So, take some time and write down your products' real "secrets." What part of the patent cannot be duplicated easily?

Next on the "real strength" list are skills and knowledge. Once the natural talent is established, of course, studying into the area, acquiring knowledge, is necessary. Then becoming skilled in the area of expertise, becoming able to use the knowledge aptly, is crucial. Finally, all of these must be wrapped in a package of passion. Without passion, nothing is pursued or finished. Do you love yourself? Are you proud? Do you feel accomplished? Do you believe that you are giving back to the world in a way that makes sense and elevates your likelihood of self-actualization? What are your feelings about the products produced by Me, Inc? As you can see, the honesty factor is critical in making these lists and assessing your talents. It is just as much of a crime to underestimate your Production Department as it is to overestimate it. We all see "unsung" talents every day and can easily pick out people who have let some of the fruits of their Production Department die on the vine.

The honest process of discovering your own strengths can be enlightening and can save life mistakes. Shortly after I graduated with my degree in psychology, I took an interest in computer programming. I absolutely loved it. But as I progressed in the department and moved on to upper level courses, I realized that I did not "have it." I was lacking the natural talent in mathematics that it takes to excel in computer programming. Yes, it was difficult to admit and yes, it was disappointing. But I believe that it would have been far more disappointing and potentially destructive to myself and to others had I ignored the truth and gone forward in this area. And during my time in this department, through the group projects, I realized that some of those mathematical "whiz kids" turned to me for team leadership and that I organized, supported and managed the team and the projects very well. Say goodbye to one life road and hello to another. I guess that is what forks in the road were made for.

The Human Resource Department – Taking Care Of Yourself

Now you know the real products, how they work, what they can do, the value. What about the other departments of Me, Inc? How does the Human Resources (HR) department stack up? Do you take care of your physical and emotional health? This is the department that Stephen Covey in his book, *The Seven Habits of Highly Effective People,* would have said was responsible for "sharpening the saw." In other words, no machine can work forever without maintenance and downtime. Do you work your machines to the point of breakdown or do you take time out for oiling and tune-ups? Does everything take a back seat to production time? Can you say "no" to the musts in life long enough to do some of the wants? Or for some of you, on the flip side, can you stop grabbing immediate gratification and "fun time" to get serious about tasks? Check your production line. Is there no fun, or maybe too much fun? A good HR department will evaluate and take action. Here are some ideas for your HR department to consider. When there is a problem, do you refer out to an expert or do you just figure it out? In a business this might be calling in an auditor to look for lost money versus having the billing department manager do it. In Me, Inc, this may be the decision to have a carpenter come in versus just buying some tools and starting to hammer. Are you able to delegate tasks or do you always try to be everything to everyone, including yourself? In a business this might be a manager staying late to do the job "right" versus taking the time to train the staff to do it right. In Me, Inc, this could be sharing power with your spouse about decisions. Can you reach out for help or do you just suffer in silence? In a business this may be the owner calling in a consultant for conflict resolution versus mediating the conflict herself. In Me, Inc this could be calling in a counselor versus just sticking your head in the sand and hoping the conflicts will go away. Do you bring in trainers and participate in continuing education or do you remain stagnant and rest on your laurels? In a business this would be sending employees for continuing education and having companywide education onsite. In Me, Inc, this is reading, taking classes and keeping up to date on issues and events that affect your life and the lives of your family members. Do you keep accurate records of interactions and engage in performance checks or do you just assume that things are moving forward? In a business, this involves keeping the minutes from meetings and making sure that everyone gets performance reviews and receives feedback. The feedback given should be based on the reviews, done on a routine basis, and be honest and useful. In Me, Inc this involves keeping records of the parts of your life and important interactions and taking "time outs" to review where you have been with your life, where you are now and where you are going. The records in Me, Inc can be in the form of a daily journal about your activities and feelings, graphs that show improvements in your activities such as exercise, weight loss, or productive discussions with significant others, or just notes that "track" anything that you believe is worth tracking.

Customer Service – Taking Care Of Others

It seems that rather than becoming stronger and better, Customer Service has diminished over the years. More and more companies are focusing on low cost goods and cutting back on service. It is sometimes difficult to find a person "on the floor" of a department store to answer questions and it has become a standing joke that when calling the support number of many companies, the telephone is answered by someone in India. But because of this trend, several companies in most industries have used the standard of lack of good service as a marketing tool and niche for their own product. They tell potential customers that they "will be there every step of the way." Fortunately for these companies, there is a large group of consumers out there who would rather pay a little more and get good service than settle for low cost.

A comparable trend has happened in the world of relationships. People want more from relationships than ever before. In the past, the typical American family consisted of a working man, a stay-at-home woman and several children. There was one family vehicle, very few extras and most people just accepted their lot in life. With technology, the growth of women's rights and education came the advent of choices and expectations. Interestingly, women's rights to work and grow gave men the right and the obligation to get in touch with their "feminine side" and talk more about feelings and become more involved in the day to day operations of the family. Relationships became an investment and the partners were expected to meet emotional needs as well as physical needs. Paradoxically, the rights to "experiment" with relationships and wait to settle down were in this new package. But some of the messages became confusing to our Customer Service Departments.

Given the strain created by today's elevated expectations, people in American families genuinely need more stress relief, understanding and comfort than they did 100 or even 50 years ago, and to a large degree, they expect it. All of the sensitivity, emotional intelligence and relationship books that are being published fill a need because of expectations that are present, but the books perhaps also have a major hand in creating the expectation and perception of the need. With all the literature and social change out there, everyone is expected to provide better "customer service," that is, caretaking of all kinds, to those close to them. Challenge yourself to consider the following. Is it more important to make more money so that you can afford to provide the family with more toys? Or is the greater importance on creating the nonworking, nonearning time to increase the chances you can really "be there" when the emotional need arises? To be present and really be a family on a regular basis as opposed to being individuals? Yes, the two can go together, but how well is your Customer Service Department really working?

Finally, Customer Service can also extend to taking care of others in the sense of looking after the well-being of your neighbors, or of doing volunteer work that contributes to the better functioning of our schools, churches, charitable organizations and the community at large. I would certainly encourage people to donate money to charities. I would contend, however, that throwing money at charitable organizations or at people close to you who have emotional needs does not qualify as good Customer Service anymore than saying to a customer with a broken lawnmower, "Here is $25, put it toward a new one." When considering community service as part of your Customer Service policies, take into account that in working with many clients over the years, I have seen that one of the contributing factors to unhappiness is lack of a "greater cause" in the lives of these clients. No matter how many gifts a person has in life, it seems that unless there is something bigger than self to contribute to, they will be unhappy and unfulfilled. I agree with Stephen Covey, who in *The Seven Habits of Highly Effective People* makes the point that our Circle of Concern, or those things that we care about, must not be much larger than our Circle of Influence, or those things that we can have an effect upon. If the Circle of Concern is vastly larger than the Circle of Influence, we will simply be anxious and unhappy about not being able to do enough. But I also believe that if we simply focus on our own lives and not on anything larger than ourselves, we will become self-consumed, unhappy and possibly hopeless. There are many issues and causes that can overwhelm us with their enormity, but there are hundreds to which individuals can contribute and for which they can do a great deal of good.

Research and Development – Improvement and Growth

What about the Research and Development (R & D) department? In a business, this department is responsible for making sure that the products get better and better as time goes on and that new products are developed as needed. In Me, Inc, this is honest appraisal of self and making constant self-improvements based on that appraisal. Do you take a good hard look at your "You" product on a regular basis, evaluate its quality, and "grow new parts" of Me, Inc? Do you make a point of using your true strengths in new ways? No matter what your vocation or profession, make sure that you seek out continuing education on a regular basis. Make sure that you get input from your peers and your supervisors and advisors about what you can learn and how you can grow. Many Me, Incs develop new interests and hobbies as they get older. This is because the product line needs to be enhanced. It helps to develop new relationships or to freshen up the old ones. Stagnation might work for a swamp, but businesses need new ideas and innovation to survive, and Me, Inc is a business.

Discussing the need to know your real strengths in the 4-1-1 on Me, Inc section above, I alluded to Marcus Buckingham and Donald Clifton's book, *Now, Discover Your Strengths*. The major purpose of this book is to acquaint you with the discovery of 34 themes of talent, the nature of those themes, and the opportunity to assess your own dominant themes or "signature strengths." The book provides you with a code to access the StrengthsFinder, an instrument you can take online which gives you a report of your five most dominant themes. From this report, the book guides you in how to explore, develop and capitalize on these strengths. Although the StrengthsFinder was developed in the workplace, the knowledge of your strengths is easily applicable to both the work and non-work lives of Me, Inc. It is an excellent place for your R & D department to begin researching and developing the best products and potential products of Me, Inc.

A major point Buckingham and Clifton make is that becoming the best you can be is *not* a matter of boosting your proficiency in weak areas. They define weakness very uniquely as "anything that gets in the way of excellent performance." Lack of talent, knowledge or skills is not a weakness unless you are called upon to function well in that area. For example, a company that makes swim suits would not consider it a weakness that they cannot fill an order for packaged cupcakes. They would, however, consider it a weakness if some of their employees were engaging in such unhealthy behaviors that the production line was shutting down twice a day.

Marketing and Sales – Promoting Me, Inc.

So far, the product is the product even if it is in a vacuum and nobody ever sees it. You exist and you are you. That is true down to your core, even if you sat home alone all of the time. Now it is time to look at what the product becomes or seems to become when the Sales Department gets involved. Every company has a Marketing and Sales Department, even if it is a "one person band." The Marketing and Sales Department of a company consists of those persons who choose a target market, determine the best pricing, tell the target market about the product, and persuade them to buy the product. This is the department that advertises the product. This is what the public sees. The "official" Sales Department can consist of front line employees, that is, service people who deal directly with customers or people who are assigned the specific duties of going out and telling people about the products and about the company. Unofficially, all employees need to be in sales. The Sales Department is absolutely critical to the success of any business. No matter what the product or its quality is, Sales and Marketing determine who will be checking out the product. If the Sales Department cannot think of anything interesting to say, the product will die on the shelf.

Anyone who can talk and who is exposed to other people becomes part of an unofficial sales force who pass on word-of-mouth information about a company's products. For this reason, the first action that I take when called in to work with a business is to institute a Code of Conduct for everyone who works there. Considering that most behavior is Top Down in a business, I work extensively with the owners and the managers to get a "buy in" on the Code of Conduct. The top people must be on board and indoctrinated to a code that states that all communications will be by the Rules of Engagement that you will encounter in Chapter 7, and that all employees will say only positive things about themselves, the company, the products and about each other. Once we have this buy-in, these top people begin to help indoctrinate the staff. This does not mean in any way that problems are ignored or that negative issues do not come up. It is just that when problems and issues arise, they must be handled by very specific rules. It also means that problems are discussed with people who can help solve them. The problems must also be discussed in such a way that everyone involved is leading from a solution orientation. Problems cannot be discussed in a "complaint session" way at the water cooler or while out drinking with friends or colleagues. This can be particularly challenging since triangulation, or gossipy talking with one person or group about another person or group, is an evolutionarily "prepared" response to compensate for low belonging feelings (I will discuss this in Chapter 4, "To Do Or Not To Do: Goal Setting Part 1").

What about the Sales Department of Me, Inc? If you were my client, you would be forbidden to say anything negative about yourself. No more, "Oh, what a jerk I am" or "I'm just a klutz," or "How stupid of me," or "You'll just be mad at me," or "I'm no good at that" or "He will just say no." There are probably a thousand other examples of negative self-statements that I forbid my clients to use. The same goes for couples and partners. They are forbidden to make negative statements about each other, unless they state them as solvable problems. The problem must also be brought up in such a way that it is clear the problem-raiser is going to be proactive in the solution process. The rule applies that the problem-raiser only speaks about such issues directly to the other person involved or in professional consultation sessions with a coach, counselor or consultant. In other words, people must be part of the solution or "shut up."

There is nothing so destructive to a company or to an individual as a Sales Department that talks negatively about the product or the company. After all, who is the public listening to about product information? If the Sales Department is talking down the product it must not be a very good product. I am sure that most of you have been at a social event and heard an acquaintance or friend talk negatively about his or her "company," whether that company is their actual workplace or their partner, family or friends. You probably thought to yourself, "I am going to make sure that I never buy anything they make (or hang out with whoever they hang out with)." Humans are always involved in self-fulfilling prophecies. We uphold the belief systems that make sense to us. Say negative remarks about yourself long enough and you will believe them deep down and you will start to make them come true. The product will get shabbier. The production line will weaken. Sales will drop off and this will reinforce the negative thinking as though the "bad luck" came first, rather than the thought driving the actions that brought on the "bad luck."

In a business, the Sales Department can be the "make it or break it" point. Even great products will disappear if there is bad press, or if there is no press. A silent Sales Department can be just as destructive as a bad one. In Me, Inc, no matter how wonderful you are, if you do not "advertise" your wares, or interact with others, nobody will ever know what you have to offer. Businesses work diligently now for "Search Engine Optimization." In other words, when a key word associated with their business is "Googled," they want to make sure that their business comes up near the top of the list. That is because they know people will be most attracted to the most obvious. So make sure that your Sales Department knows your other departments very well and knows all of your key words and that at some level Sales "puts them out there." As I tell clients, and my children, "There is no guarantee that you will get to where you want to be even if you have everything right, but there is a guarantee that you will *not* get there if your own advertising says that you will not."

Me, Inc Through and Through – Authenticity

Now comes a critical factor. Do the Sales Department and the

Production Department match? What happens when the Production Department is making a shabby product and the Sales Department is saying it is the greatest product of its kind in the world? What happens when the Sales Department says that the product can "virtually fly a plane" when in fact the starter motor does not turn over the engine? What happens when the Sales Department says there is great "after purchase" support and in fact there is no Customer Service department? What happens if Sales says there is a "buy one, get one free" this week and forgets to tell Production to step up its output, or if Sales promises a warranty that Production cannot afford? What are the customers or clients of this company going to do? Probably go away or take action against the company. They are certainly not going to become advocates of this company and its products. But even subtle mismatches between Sales and Production adversely affect a business. I work with physicians and mental health providers, who are both in fields where traditionally the public expects them not to care about money. It is obvious with many of these professionals that there is angst around this issue. They of course want to make a basic living, and since wanting "more" is a built-in desire, they of course also like doing well financially. When it comes time to talk about money or to set prices with their patients, however, they are usually very uncomfortable. Unfortunately, this discomfort is seen by their clients as "something wrong," even though what is wrong is not easily determinable. The tone of "something wrong" is probably conveyed subtly by the professional's uneasiness in such moments as when the doctor must prescribe a test or procedure that he or she knows will involve an out-of-pocket cost for the patient. Whenever the customer or client senses something wrong, it can only mean bad news for the company.

What about Me, Inc? Check out your Sales Department. Does it match your Production department? What is Sales telling the world about your product? Are you honest about your product? Are you selling a Volkswagen but touting a Cadillac? Are you making bold statements about your courage while you are shaking in your boots? Are you making promises that you cannot or will not keep? Do you "put on a good front" to convince people that you are more than you really believe you are? Are you covering up feelings of inadequacy with inflated claims or actions? Your body will usually speak from your Production Department, while your words have been designed and orchestrated by the Sales Department. Remember that first we are animals before we are humans. Even when the information is not used "mindfully," people still smell fear and other emotions and they do use the information to make decisions, the same way a dog does. It is what is called "gut instinct" because there are wires directly from the gut to the brain. We still have this enteric system, just as our other animal friends have. If you are interested in this topic more, read Gavin De Becker's *Protecting the Gift* or *The Gift of Fear*. Add to this, that a large portion of what you convey will be coming from your body. The person who is listening will most certainly believe what your body is saying over what your words are saying. Or they will just sense that something is not quite right, and shy away.

When your Sales and Production Departments do not match and the mismatch makes people uncomfortable, it is most likely that they will assume it means something bad. And unless they are incredibly assertive, they will probably just avoid you or make a mental note not to trust you anymore. You will be unlikely to ever receive feedback on how you gave them a mixed message. Business owners and managers pay consultants a great deal of money for what they call a "360," or an honest view of themselves from the people around them. Think about the people that you know who are under the illusion that they are good at something when in fact the rest of the world believes otherwise. I recently experienced a good example of this phenomenon when I was approached at the end of a communication workshop by a woman who had chosen to take the session opposite mine. She boldly stated that she did not need my workshop because she is already very good at communication. I happen to know this woman from several professional groups and therefore have had the opportunity to observe her communication skills. Unfortunately, she has not hired me nor taken the time to get a "360." No matter how uncomfortable you may think it will be, have the courage to get a "360" on yourself. Just make sure that it comes from people who really care about you and not from anyone who may have a hidden agenda. And, when it comes to the Sales and Production Departments not matching, remember the old saying, "A picture is worth a thousand words." The picture is your actions, and actions always speak louder than words.

What do you do when Sales and Production do not match? It depends on the reason. If a man is telling some young girl that he loves her so that she will have sex with him, he should go take a cold shower, slap himself in the face, go to confession and look into becoming a monk. If, however, you are telling a potential boss that she should hire you because you are very qualified while believing that you just don't have it, go and re-evaluate, get some feedback from people who genuinely care about you, and get help to either pursue another career or build your self-esteem enough to believe in yourself.

No Room For the Emperor

Finally, do not be the Emperor! Remember the story about the Emperor who went around with no clothes on while everyone in the Kingdom pretended he was clothed? One day at a ceremony, a very assertive young man pointed out that the Emperor was not dressed. It was not politically correct, but it sure was the right thing to say. Are you or anyone you know trying to be the Emperor? It involves pretending that you are something that you are not and expecting everyone around you to support the fantasy. This is very common in people who have unmet belonging needs and are trying to fit into groups that are not right for them. These individuals are so anxious to belong somewhere and to be loved that they grab onto a group and pretend to have the characteristics that they believe this "tribe" finds desirable. The pattern can become so deeply ingrained that the individual loses track of what he or she really likes and dislikes. This person cannot stand the pain and insecurity of not belonging long enough to find the right group, so the nakedness gets denied and anger is the reaction to anyone who points out the lack of clothing. The pattern and type of person is demonstrated delightfully in a popular movie from a few years ago, *Runaway Bride*. Julia Roberts plays a woman who has been engaged to three men, but each time she runs away at the wedding. Richard Gere is investigating her and at one point asks her what kind of eggs she likes. She cannot answer the question and he confronts her with the fact that he has already checked into this issue. He knows that each time she was with a new man, she ate her eggs however the man ate his eggs. She had lost herself by being so intent on gaining his approval and on belonging to his "tribe."

A variation on the Emperor Pattern is also seen in what I refer to as "Bleacher Sitters." These are the individuals who are so afraid of the "monsters" in their minds (refer to Chapter 4, the first Goal Setting chapter) that they never enter the race. There they sit on the bleachers, watching the event pass them by. Yes, they say that they will step in when the field is dry or when there are not quite so many others on the track or when the competition is less or when they are better performers, but it never gets quite perfect enough for them. These Emperors lack the courage to go shopping and buy the outfits that they need. They do not have what it takes to display their true colors boldly, to risk being ridiculed for not getting it right. So they go naked. But they also are absent the courage to admit that they failed and missed the shopping trip, so they pretend and expect others to pretend. This is a loss, both to the Emperors and Bleacher Sitters and to the world.

As you can see, all of the departments of Me, Inc serve a function and are vital to the success of the business. Making sure that they are all on the same page creates a stable, honest company that will become better over time and will certainly be a better "parent company."

If you are one of the Bleacher Sitters, you are probably overly cautious and this makes business ownership very difficult. Entrepreneurs need to be able to risk loss and failure. Of course, these risks can be taken with some caution and thoughtfulness, but successful people do not stay safe all of the time. Sometimes a business owner "puts a product out there" that he or she is not sure of and it gets slammed down. But as Thomas Edison said after creating hundreds of bad light bulbs, "I now know many ways to not make a light bulb." His Sales Department did not apologize. Instead, they cheered his Production Department on and as I write these words in my well-lit office, I know how that story ended. So, if your Sales Department needs some help to root for Production, go talk to some people who love you and whom you trust, or go get a professional to talk with. Your departments need to be united and they need to be willing to risk others seeing the product and, with appropriate caution, taking the chances that may invite failure and loss. Those same people who help you unite your departments and take risks can be invaluable for support and guidance when a product fails or needs some tweaking.

If you are an Emperor, it means you do not have faith in your product or that you do not *love* your company and its product. This is not hopeless. Maybe it is just that the "target market" is wrong. When a good product is being sold to the wrong group, it can look as bad as a bad product. For example, most of us just love ice cream, but imagine setting up your new ice cream stand next to the offices of the American Association of the Lactose Intolerant. Some business owners would go to the R & D Department and suggest that a new product line be developed that can be enjoyed by the lactose intolerant. Many more businesses would just say, "Wrong market, let's go find the right one." Evaluate those with whom you are associating and to whom you are trying to "sell yourself." Ask yourself some or all of the following questions: "Do I really like this group? Deep down, do I want to hang with these people? Do we have the same beliefs and philosophies? Even if our beliefs match, is there some uncomfortable style clash? Can I be authentic with these people and still feel like part of the group?" If any of the answers are "no," then re-evaluate. Do you need to change your core beliefs? For example, if the group is filled with people who are self-confident and you are hiding your deep self-doubts, then maybe the group will be fine for you when Me, Inc hires a consultant to upgrade its self-image. But if the group likes to hunt and kill small animals and you are hiding the fact that you are an animal rights advocate, then the product is fine, but Sales needs to find another target market.

Some Final Words On Optimizing Performance and Interdepartmental Cooperation

I find an imagery exercise very helpful in the process of "department research." Design a place in your mind that you love. It can be a house or a spot in nature, a favorite room or even a boat. It must be a place that you feel safe and serene and it must be of your own design. So if it is based on a place that actually exists, modify it some and make it your own perfect, personal place. Once you have become comfortable with the place and you find just thinking about it very relaxing, start to invite your departments in. Make sure that every part of your Self feels safe and that there is no danger of being shunned, put down or otherwise disrespected. If you listen to the parts of yourself, you will discover over time all of the departments that you have and you will be able to accurately assess what Me, Inc has to offer and where it needs help. In this exercise, assume that you have all the departments, including Production (what you really do in the world, who you really are), HR (Human Resources, the ways in which you take care of yourself), Customer Service (your integrity and the ways in which you take care of those close to you and your community at large), R & D (Research and Development, ways in which you improve yourself and engage in personal growth), and Marketing and Sales (ways in which you portray yourself to the world around you). Be sure that each department has at least a "representative," a voice, at this gathering, or perhaps all the "staff" of all the departments are invited. Some of the departments may look understaffed, under-budgeted, "faking it" (trying to look better than they are, Emperor-style) or poorly functioning. This is, however, part of the information you are gathering, information about work within yourself that is needed. So do not judge the information as good or bad, but merely take it in as information. Each department has a voice and must be respected, but be sure the agenda is that decisions are to be made "for the greater good of all." And be sure there is a CLO at this and any future meetings, to conduct the meeting by rules of order and ensure the safety of all parties. That is your "overseeing" part. Brainstorming and "wild ideas" are invited and can be expressed without fear of reproach. Most of them will never be expressed outside of this closed meeting, but this open forum for expression will give birth to the ideas that become the greatest of Me, Inc.

I have focused on the critical importance of authenticity as portrayed by how well the Production Department and the Sales and Marketing Department match. Authenticity is critically important in business and in life, however, and inauthenticity can come from any department. R & D may be announcing proudly that they are moving in this or that new direction, but what actions and concrete evidence proves that the movement is taking place? Your Customer Service department may be absolutely convinced that they are taking great care of the people closest to them, but is this the feedback you are getting (or would get if you asked) from the people under your care? HR may be quite assured that they are taking good care of you, and may even be able to list visible activities, such as working out or spending ample time with friends, that prove it. But the key test here is to ask, "Do I *feel* well cared for?" And remember, HR is not expected to go it alone, as we especially emphasize in Chapter 9 on support systems. One of HR's legitimate activities is linking up and collaborating with other people's Customer Service departments.

Chapter 3

SWOT First, Plan Next: Business Plans for Me, Inc and We, Inc

We know that a business can't be run without a plan.
It simply is a given, so don't try to duck it, man!
A business run without a plan will be a disaster,
But a plan based on misguided goals can crash even faster.

Give me an S, for Strengths that's your foundation.
And a W for Weaknesses that lead to consternation.
Opportunities many and we hope Threats not a lot.
When we bring them all together, the analysis is SWOT.

For business, individual and family all the same
The goals and information form a plan for the game.
With your departmental ducks all neatly in a row,
In the race of life you're at the line and good to GO!

The Plain White Rapper

Once the leaders of a business know all of the departments and their functions and really understand "the guts" of the organization, it is time to set some goals. But the prequel to "The Attack of the Goal Setters" is "SWOT Strikes First," or a SWOT Analysis. SWOT is an acronym for Strengths, Weaknesses, Opportunities and Threats.

A Business Example

Let's first look at the SWOT analysis of a small business that provides mental health services to individuals and couples and also provides business coaching and consulting to multiple-owner businesses. The SWOT analysis of this business might look like Figure 3.1.

Figure 3.1
SWOT Analysis Of A Small Business

STRENGTHS	WEAKNESSES
1. One owner is a licensed Psychologist 2. Accept all insurances for mental health services 3. Mental health background gives owners a vast knowledge of human behavior, motivation and change 4. Research and evidence-based philosophy 5. Well established in the community 6. Called by the media as experts 7. Ability to work by telephone and in others' spaces – a market without boundaries 8. Experience with medical professionals and physicians – a niche 9. Provide a wide range of assessments	1. Mental health background is sometimes a stigma for clients 2. Insurance slant can create "in the box thinking" by some clients 3. Owners married to each other – can cause boundary problems 4. Dependency on mental health practice to feed coaching and assessment practice 5. One owner has little motivation to grow or change the practice 6. Low marketing budget
OPPORTUNITIES	**THREATS**
1. Businesses need our services 2. World is becoming more interested in emotional intelligence 3. Expanding to work with attorneys 4. Clients are willing to provide testimonials to use to approach other businesses 5. Offering assessments to other therapists for their clients 6. Medical professionals' performance ratings can be improved with assessments and communication training	1. Managed care which insurance companies can always tighten 2. Dependency on insurance companies with sometimes unfavorable changes in that industry 3. Stiff competition in business consulting 4. Public sees mental health experts as "only therapists" 5. Geographic area is slow to progress 6. Current economic downturn

It is important for the SWOT analysis to be brutally honest. Therefore, at first glance, the analysis in some cases may look ominous and could create a potential for pessimism if the strengths are few and the weaknesses and threats are many. It is important to note here that keeping a goal-setting, solution-oriented mentality is critical for this process to be productive. It is also important to note that the theme of some items emerges in more than one category. For example, the Strength of accepting all insurances for mental health services carries with it the Weaknesses of stigma and narrow thinking and the Threats of managed care procedures and dependency on insurance.

Your perspective can also be a factor when deciding into which category an item fits. There is the old story of the pessimistic shoe sales person who went market researching in an African country and reported back to his boss, "There is no potential for a market here, since no one wears shoes." The optimistic sales person, reporting back from the same country, exclaimed, "What a great market! No one's got any shoes!" Look at the companies that make the ripped jeans. Obviously at some point they observed that young people like to wear their jeans torn. Rather than lamenting, a clever business person decided to sell pre-torn jeans and through creative marketing and partnering with celebrities, they actually turned the jeans into a very expensive designer item. The designer jeans genius and the optimistic shoe sales person reshaped their observations into opportunities. So in my Figure 3.1 example, I focused on the "boundary problems" created by the business partners being married. An example of such a boundary issue might be that the couple gets confused on when to stop talking business and become more personal with each other. Viewed from this angle, the business partners being married is classified as a Weakness. If instead the focus had been on, say, "it is always easy for the partners to consult on business matters," the married status would have been categorized as a Strength. If in looking at your SWOT analysis, others see some of your Weaknesses or Threats as Strengths, then it may be a signal that you are being pessimistic, looking at the dark side and missing some obvious or subtle light shining through.

Some Weaknesses are thought of as characteristics or longstanding traits, of an individual or a business, that are unlikely to change and that we therefore choose to accept and then adapt to or work around. In this case, the "mental health background" Weakness is a piece of unchangeable history (but note that it also appears as a Strength when looked at from a different angle). The "insurance slant" Weakness is unlikely to change as long as mental health services are a mainstay of the business, and a large portion of the business income relies on insurance. And if the owner who has "little motivation to grow or change the practice" is this way because he or she, by nature, just likes the gauge to stay on "status quo," then this will not prove to be a highly changeable trait. But some other Weaknesses in the example can be seen as opportunities in disguise. If the Weakness of the "low marketing budget" can be ramped up a modest amount, Opportunities are created for developing other markets, such as the businesses of attorneys, other therapists and medical professionals. This eliminates the Weakness of the coaching and assessment practice being dependent on the mental health practice for referrals. The new Opportunity might be described as "increase marketing budget and time allocation to develop new feeders and referral sources to the coaching and assessment business." Sometimes, also, a Threat can be turned to advantage. A major economic downturn can be ominous for any business. But what if mental health, coaching and assessment services can help other businesses and individuals become more robust, resilient and likely to survive the downturn? Then with proper marketing, the downturn becomes an Opportunity.

Personal and Family Examples

Now, in Figure 3.2, let us look at the SWOT self-analysis by Tom, a single-man Me, Inc.

Figure 3.2
SWOT Analysis Of Tom's Me, Inc

STRENGTHS	**WEAKNESS**
1. Good paying job 2. Young 3. Good attention to detail, love data, analysis, budgeting, etc. 4. Steady, conscientious, good at following through once a task is set in motion 5. Great first-impression and contact maker 6. Sense of humor	1. Limited education (one year college) 2. Limited support and reality testing from others 3. Little experience with and some aversion to new ventures 4. Often shy away from deepening a relationship once initial contact has been made
OPPORTUNITIES	**THREATS**
1. Was recently offered a move into management at work 2. Management training available could help develop and call forth my leadership and risk-taking qualities 3. Long-term relationship is ready to be taken to the marriage planning level	1. Poor economy 2. Mother in poor health 3. Partner in long-term relationship has threatened to leave if relationship does not progress to deeper level of commitment

Of course your SWOT chart will be based on the departments in your Me, Inc. For example, do you want your HR department to be very strong? How many friend departments do you have or want? What does the department that has parents in it look like? Do you do community service and if so, do you really value it?

It becomes obvious that SWOT charts are not stagnant. Good businesses do a SWOT Analysis every two to three years, or even more often when changes occur. We live in a fast-changing world. For example, a company that made vinyl records could have listed "well-made products" as one of its Strengths, but once cassette tapes, then CDs, then iPods came into being, it did not matter how well-made the obsolete vinyl records were.

Let's take a look at some of the changes in the SWOT Analysis when Figure 3.2 Tom's Me, Inc, becomes Tom and Mary's We, Inc. The points in bold below are new factors that arose or became relevant as a result of moving from a Me, Inc to a 4-person We, Inc.

Figure 3.3
SWOT Analysis Of Tom and Mary's We, Inc

STRENGTHS	WEAKNESSES
1. Tom has well paying job, with recent development of his management, leadership and risk-taking capacities 2. Still young 3. Tom loves job 4. Mary able to stay at home with kids 5. **Supportive partners (can bounce ideas and feelings off each other)** 6. **Shared sense of humor makes life easier, laughter relieves tension** 7. **Partners love how each takes care of details, follow-through**	1. Limited education (1½years of college between us) 2. Mary not earning money 3. **Children are young and dependent** 4. **Increase in expenses** 5. **Both partners are detail-oriented so sometimes we compete for the same tasks and fail to see the big picture** 6. **We are both risk-avoidant in our personal lives and often fail to move forward when necessary** 7. **Television draws too much attention away from family interactions**
OPPORTUNITIES	THREATS
1. Use more of the management, leadership and risk-taking skills from work in home life 2. **Meet other parents** 3. **Tom could open up, talk more about feelings and issues with Mary** 4. **Savings and dual incomes may allow return to school OR move to new neighborhood, but not both**	1. Poor economy 2. **Drug dealer who lives in the neighborhood** 3. **Substandard schools** 4. **Since Tom's mother died, his father is more of a presence in our lives than we feel comfortable with**

Getting Deeply Involved With SWOT

The points made from the business example apply to the Me, Inc and the We, Inc cases, too. With the right attitude and viewpoint, some Weaknesses and even some Threats are convertible to Opportunities. The "children are young and dependent" Weakness can also present the Opportunity to expand the friendship and support networks through connecting with other parents. The ongoing Weakness of "limited education," becomes a possible Opportunity within the setting of the family's pooled resources. Some Threats, such as the neighborhood drug dealer and the substandard schools may be a call to be very creative in the search for Opportunities.

Two additional points can be drawn from this example. First, even if it is not the original intention, many Opportunities will end up addressing some Weaknesses or Threats. If Tom takes the Opportunity of opening up and talking more with his wife, Mary, that in itself will mean he is being less risk-avoidant. They will then both probably be more likely to see the big picture and to find ways to cope with the increased expenses, thus addressing three Weaknesses. The second point is that often a Strength, like having a "well paying job," becomes an Opportunity when applied in a new way, such as the ability to invest or start one's own business.

The more you work with SWOT, the more it will take on a holistic, ecological and organic life of its own. You will become adept at seeing the connections among the four cells, as in the examples above. And like a whole, organic being, the nature and the workings among the parts change over time. Note how the Threat of a sickly mother in the Me, Inc SWOT (Figure 3.2), has morphed into a new Threat, an intrusive father (Figure 3.3), by the time Mom is gone and we arrive at We, Inc a few years later. The steadiness, conscientiousness and follow-through Strengths of Figure 3.2, Me, Inc, still show up as Strengths in Figure 3.3, We, Inc as "Partners love how each takes care of details, follow-through." But they have also become a Weakness because both partners sometimes fail to see the "big picture."

Note that Mary's being able to be at home with the kids is a Strength because of what it offers to the family quality, but it is also a Weakness because of the lack of a second income. SWOT provides a way to see very clearly those items that need to be carefully weighed by asking such questions as, "Is this more valuable as a Strength than it is detrimental as a Weakness?" The tool not only helps to see the value of mindfulness and close self-examination in managing our Me, Incs and our We, Incs, it also helps in the process of achieving this self-awareness.

Over time, Strengths endure, and can be made to grow if properly placed and not overplayed. The Strength of Tom's "sense of humor" in

Me, Inc, Figure 3.2, has become a "shared sense of humor" in Figure 3.3, We, Inc, that helps the couple and family through rough spots. To have the energy and focus to cultivate and team up on Strengths, however, we must avoid the mistake many people make of trying to fortify Weaknesses beyond what is necessary. If a master statistician who is unable to teach takes a position at a university where she is required to teach, she will definitely need to read some books or get some coaching on how to convey her statistical brilliance to others. But the very shy people of the world are wasting their time if they are striving to become superstar extroverts. Similarly, the quiet, unassuming employee who just wants to do assigned jobs with clear expectations should not aspire to become the inspirational leader of the company. Mainly we do best to work around our Weaknesses and develop and capitalize on our Strengths.

SWOT and Goal-Setting

SWOT analysis is not only critical to the process of goal setting, but it also helps to determine what the goals are. If under Weaknesses in Figure 3.3, the drug dealer or the substandard schools are out of control, then We, Inc. might do well to set a goal of moving out of the area. If the job under Strengths is very well paying and Tom loves his work enough, then staying with the company and investigating all of the Opportunities may become a very definite goal of We, Inc.

One of the factors that can show up during a SWOT Analysis is the power structure of Me, Inc and We, Inc. Knowing this can change the goal statements in the goal setting process. For example, let us say that a We, Inc SWOT lists "Take-charge partner" under Strengths. Under Weaknesses, it may not be surprising to see "One partner's opinions are not heard." The take-charge partner is taking charge so strongly that he or she is not allowing the other partner to have a voice. If so, then the issue of power differentials may become a priority goal. This goal only came to the surface, however, because the person wrote down both edges of this double-edged sword.

The SWOT Analysis is a very good start for differentiating between short-term and long-term goals. Read the two chapters on goal setting though, before you actually set any goals. Make sure, if you are a We, Inc, that your partner and depending upon their ages, your children are involved. While it is a bad idea to give children the idea that they "run the show," they are a major part of the family dynamics and make great contributions to family discussions and plans. In fact, this process requires some real balance. Many years ago, children did not have any input at all, giving rise to the saying, "Children should be seen and not heard". Those times were full of a certain darkness, with children, for example, who did not report abuse or were not believed when they did. Unfortunately, the pendulum has swung too far the other way. Many children now think that they are the center of the universe, and are given far too much power to influence family decisions and how family time is spent. Children can become both narcissistic and insecure when they are allowed too much input into the process of running a household. We should seek to operate in moderation and with the clear understanding that the family is not a democracy, where everyone has equal influence. It should usually be a gentle and loving republic, where voices are heard but do not always have a vote. Sometimes it must act as an outright dictatorship, for example, when mature decisions must be made quickly. Given these understandings and ground rules, children can be an incredibly valuable asset to processes like SWOT analysis. They have a tendency to be very honest and to see things without many of the biases adults collect along the way. When children feel safe and listened to, they will tell you and show you what they need and where you and the family need improvements.

Meetings

Successful businesses often have Strategic Planning Retreats to work on SWOT and goal setting. The retreat is then followed up with regular meetings to update the goals and to measure the success. This model can translate very well to Me, Inc and We, Inc. If you are a Me, Inc, then set aside time on a regular basis to "meet with yourself." Make sure that you are in a quiet, undisturbed environment. This is not the time for a Vegas excursion. If you are a We, Inc, then you need two different types of meetings, one with the other adult in the household and one with the whole family. As with any meeting that you hope will be productive, have an agenda and a time limit for the meeting. The universal questions are, "Where have I (we) been? Where am I (are we) now? Where am I (are we) going?" Some other universals that have proven very productive for my clients are: each person stating something that they like about each of the other people and something that they like about the life they are living; each person being given the opportunity, without the fear of criticism, to state something that they would like changed; and each person stating something that they want to improve in themselves and if necessary asking for help and support in this self-improvement.

Of course the age of any children present will dictate to some degree the length of the We, Inc family meetings. But regardless of the age of the children, these meetings should not drag out. Meetings without limits become aimless and can lapse into chat or gripe sessions. When participants know they only have from 3:30 to 4:30 to get business done, they tend to be much more focused. And remember that even when you become a We, Inc, you are still always a Me, Inc, too. So, keep up your Me, Inc "meetings with yourself" in addition to any We, Inc meetings.

Once the practice of the Me, Inc and We, Inc meetings has been established, it can be especially productive to have occasional retreats for the SWOT meetings. Interspersing planning and organizational meetings with sunshine or swimming or other relaxing activities can be rejuvenating and productive. Keep in mind though, that exciting and loud vacation spots are not conducive to family processing and progress. Keep it calm and mindful.

If children start this process young enough, they are automatically indoctrinated into strategic planning thinking. When they are adults, they will run their families more efficiently and they will be prepared to step into business or government seamlessly. The process automatically builds in "quality time." It encourages self- and other-exploration and understanding. It builds in conflict resolution. Even though We, Inc is not always a democracy, this process builds in the learning of the value and methods of individual input and power. As the children get older, they have more and more input and the process of sharing power becomes natural and comfortable. All of the other tools in *CLO* are incorporated into the SWOT and the strategic planning, so your "direct reports" (the children) will have learned how to make decisions using cost-benefit analyses and how to use all of the tools in the next chapters.

Leaders need to have vision and be able to see what everyone has in *common*, so that they can unite the individual clans or factions. Managers, on the other hand, need to be able to supervise and to see what each of us can offer that is *unique*. In We, Inc, parents must be both good leaders and good managers. So, what better gift could you give your direct reports than the capacity to be the best managers and leaders of their Me, Incs and of their future We, Incs?

To Connect More or Less? To Stay and Fight or To Retreat?

Everyone has Weaknesses. In the big picture, though, it is important to address only those that really matter and let some of them just "be." For example, the Weakness of managing time so poorly that nothing is ever accomplished, or the Weakness of drinking too much alcohol, will need to be "fixed." The Weakness of not being able to repair broken plumbing should probably just be overlooked (unless of course you are a plumber). A healthy SWOT analysis will have many Strengths and Opportunities, some Weaknesses and very few Threats. When there are too many Threats, a major overhaul might be necessary. Preemptive strikes may be needed in order to avoid catastrophe later. For example, a "Mom and Pop" drug store in an area that is being swallowed up by mega-stores may be clever to liquidate before they just get buried. Sometimes waiting too long to bail out or retreat can mean disaster. Watching one's Threats can be a valuable barometer of the future. If each year there are more Threats in your SWOT, check to see if a theme emerges. Are all of the Threats related to a geographic area? Are they all related to a relationship that Me, Inc is in or an ongoing problem that We, Inc has? Once you ascertain a theme, you will be able to apply the rules and tools from the next chapters to adopt a solution orientation and to proceed toward a solution.

One hint: The most common theme of Threats and Weaknesses from within Me, Inc or We, Inc is that of faulty communication and human interconnection. By far the most common issue single individuals have is social isolation. By far the most common problem couples and families have is faulty communication methods or the refusal of some or all parties to communicate. Fear, whether reality-based or not, is another common underlying theme. Sometimes when a Me, Inc or a We, Inc has excessive Threats, it is because there is some fear-based payoff to the person or a "monster in the mind" at the center of the Threats. Assess very carefully what the causes of your Threats are. Let us say, for example, that the partner who is responsible for earning the money of We, Inc is too afraid of rejection to look for another job and the family cannot afford to move away from their present rough neighborhood because of this. Then the payoff to this partner is avoiding the possible pain of rejection, but this "monster in the mind" Weakness must "take a back seat" to the very real Threat.

Chapter 4

To Do Or Not To Do: Goal-Setting Part 1

You start by doing a SWOT Analysis.
Don't let the plan turn into paralysis.
Every time you pick up a book on goals,
There are the same old hows, they're just re-soles.

When you learn about the way we belong to tribes,
To the new "why" thinking you will subscribe.
Most reasons for goals aren't learned or styled,
They're instinctual, like *The Call of the Wild*.

On the flip side of the coin are the reasons we miss,
Then goals have holes like cheese that is Swiss.
Be honest about what you really want
And you will become a goal savant.

The Plain White Rapper

Successful companies make strategic plans, and from these plans they set written goals. Both of these components are critical to the successful attainment of the company goals.

But this formula is the easy part. If achieving goals were as easy as following the rule "the shortest distance between two points is a straight line," as straightforward as implementing reverse engineering and tracking daily key performance indicators, we would all be meeting or exceeding our goals every minute. Unfortunately it gets a bit more complicated than having a great list of "how tos." Take a look for a moment at an area where there are probably more "how to" formulae and experts than the world could ever need, that of healthy eating and exercise. Could there really be anyone left out there who does not know (or at least have access to the knowledge of) how to lose weight, keep the weight off and keep their bodies in good physical shape? It seems unlikely. Most of us can recite in our sleep the dos and do nots in this area. And yet, the United States now has an all-time high obesity rate and other alarming statistics such as those on high blood pressure and diabetes, even in our children. It is obvious that this is not due to lack of knowledge. It is time to look deeper.

Why First, Then How

To understand goal-setting, it is necessary to look more at the *whys* than the *hows*. As illustrated by the obesity and health picture, most people are not "getting it." Let's take a look at what we mean by the whys and the hows. The hows, of course, are the list of behaviors that need to be done, or the steps that need to be taken, in order to get from point A (where we are right now) to point B (where we say we want to be). The whys are the reasons we would or would not take these steps. They are much more powerful and important than the items on the "how" list. Goal-setting is another area where experts have come out of the woodwork to give advice and show us "systems" for goal-setting. Once I get those pesky "whys" out of the way in this chapter, then in the next chapter I will gladly be one of those experts and list what I refer to in my workshops as "Psych-cess" steps.

If you want to understand what makes an individual person tick, it is best to start with the universal truths about human behavior, those principles that make the whole species tick. I always find it most enlightening to do this from an anthropological viewpoint. This way, everyone in the group can relate immediately. The theory you are about to read is based on The Hierarchy of Needs developed by Abraham Maslow. It was a great launching point for how humans develop their needs, but I have redesigned it based on my years of working with individuals, couples and families. Once you understand how humans develop and the prioritizing of needs that takes place in this development, it is much easier to see where and how people "get stuck" at certain levels, depending on whether their needs were adequately met during their development and whether they *believe* their needs are being met currently.

A Prehistoric Story

Consider that we are animals first, and that we are very social animals. Take a trip back in time thousands of years to our beginnings as identifiably human creatures. Travel back to cave-person days when we lived in more obvious tribes than today, when we were hunters living side by side with wild animals. Survival depended on cunning and stamina, but mostly on the strength of the tribe. What were the beliefs and behaviors that contributed to survival? The answer to this question is the root of what motivates human behavior. Be there now, so through imagination you can understand and live the vital importance of the questions, "Which tribe do I belong to?" and "What is my status in the tribe?"

Your belongingness in the tribe dictates your survival even before you are born. When you were a fetus inside your mother's womb, she needed to belong and have a position within the tribe in order for you to even be born, because if she was not protected and provided for by the tribe, she did not live to breed. Following your birth, your parents needed to continue to belong and have a place in the circle of the tribe around the fire in order for you to be protected and fed and kept warm and dry. These basic physiological needs were all dependent on your parents' belonging to the tribe and therefore indirectly to your belonging status. They needed the tribe to be saying, "We love you, so we love your offspring, too." Your parents' place around the circle gives you, as part of their family, a place, too. If your parents continue to belong and to meet your needs lovingly and caringly, then you can move up to other needs. This is of course assuming that your parents have a *decent* place in the tribe and that they are treated respectfully and their basic needs are being met. We will discuss later what happens when the place in the tribe is threatened. Once you feel secure in your place with your immediate family and begin developing trust through repeated experiences of having your needs met, you begin to notice what others are saying about you and how they are looking at you and responding to you. If you continue to belong and the other members of the tribe welcome your talk and give you positive feedback and encouragement, then their esteem, along with that of your immediate family, can be forged into self-esteem. If others are careful to be honest with you about your accomplishments and to love you through "bad behavior," but not accept that type of behavior, then you develop warranted self-esteem. You come to know those talents in which you have genuine skill, and those in which you need to improve, and you are able to accept the need to improve without having negative feelings about yourself. At some point in the process, probably following some feat of strength or rite of passage, it is made clear to you that you not only have, but have *earned* your own spot around the tribal circle. While still being a part of and needing the small tribe of your immediate family, you are also your own member of the large tribe and a member of several other smaller tribes with your age peers and members with whom you share common interests and activities. Somewhere along the line you have left your parents' laps and became welcome as a real member of the larger tribe and sub-tribes. If you continue to belong, the tribe's esteem and your self-esteem allow you to try new things and experiment with some risks while remaining healthy and self-loving. You come to respect the members of your tribe and you come to care about community service. You start to move up the hierarchy of needs to the more spiritual needs of giving to the community. You begin to self-actualize.

Core Features

Looking back on this example, we can see clearly how the need to belong encompassed and provided for every other need. It was there every minute throughout the developmental history. Nobody in the tribe could survive without belonging. They all needed each other desperately in order to go on. Without people to hunt and people to cook and people to guard the cave entrance and people to watch over the children, the tribe is quickly consumed by wild animals, starves or freezes to death, or is invaded successfully by another tribe.

If you doubt the importance of belonging or the interconnectedness which is necessary for the survival of the human social animal, look at the research on infant mortality and attachments. As early as 1926, Henry Dwight Chapin provided evidence that infants who were otherwise cared for but not touched, died. Later, in 1978, Mary Salter Ainsworth and her associates provided more up-to-date evidence gathered by more sophisticated methods showing again the need for connection and touch in surviving and coping adaptively with novel, "strange" situations. So, even infants who have all of the physical needs met die when they are not touched and loved. Look also at the only commonality that investigators have found among the school shootings. The shooters were all "outcasts" of some sort. They did not belong and they lacked social support. They were all getting their physical needs met, but that hardly tells the whole story, or even the most important part of the story.

It is clear that beyond belonging, physical safety is the next need. If you get eaten by a wild animal, no other need matters. Once safety is provided, the next need is for water, food and shelter. To validate the accuracy of this sequence, take a look at physical responses to threat. Imagine being ravenously hungry. As you walk into your favorite restaurant, a grizzly bear or a serial killer greets you. Check out your body. Your digestive system in fact shuts down when you are threatened. Your blood flow is diverted to the large muscles of your arms and legs, so you are prepared to engage in fight or flight. Fighting or running will delay your favorite meal, but thoughts of this meal occupy no space in your mind at this moment. The choice of fighting or running, however, may make it possible to have a next meal, to survive. Is it safe to say that your hunger just took a back seat to your physical safety need?

After the basic physical needs, there comes the need for psychological safety. As the next two sections will make clear, psychological safety involves such components as being understood and listened to, having the ability and opportunity to gather more of the essentials of life (including mastery of skills), and being acknowledged by others as "right." Beyond psychological safety comes the need for the esteem of others (obtained in part by frequent occasions of being hailed as "right") and for internalized esteem (self-esteem or self-approval).

Some individuals attain a status we call self-actualization, being driven and guided by "doing what is truly them," "being the best they can be" and usually involving "giving back" to the world, living and acting with a sense of community and humanitarianism. An early, basic form of giving back is being helpful and listening to others in your tribe on an everyday basis, providing them with what I will show is the *core* need to be listened to and understood.

Built-In Knowledge

Let us bring this model into the modern world. We have the knowledge of our ancestors inside of us at birth, and then we spend the first several years of our life totally dependent on others, with belonging being equivalent to life itself.

So if we can acknowledge the cave person within us, with all those basic survival needs and their intensity, we can *recognize and appreciate* all the knowledge we have as beings almost from the moment of birth, due to thousands of years of evolution. We know that we need to belong to a tribe in order to survive, or in order to get any of our other needs met. We know that we need a warm, dry place to sleep and hide out from danger. We know that we need fresh water close to our "digs." We know that it is best to have some stored food in case of a shortage. So the more "things" we have, the safer we are from shortages and spoilages. We know that we need to be "right" in some sense, and validated as right, when we give critical information to our tribe. Even bees have a "dance" that they do to let their tribe know where food sources are. Critical is not too strong a word for the importance of getting the tribe's attention and making sure that the information is correct. And here is a key point. When, for example, we tell the tribe an enemy tribe is approaching, before we can be recognized as right, we must be *listened to*. So another part of the built-in knowledge we have as modern people is that we need to be listened to in order for the tribe to know us and respect our skills. If in those cave-days we developed a special talent for recognizing signs of the presence of a hungry predator, that talent would count for little if the tribe failed to listen to us when we warned them of the danger. One of the most important qualities in good managers, salespeople, teachers and counselors is empathy, or listening with understanding. I believe the vital importance of this skill is rooted in our evolution. Those individuals who were listened to had those skills essential to survival reinforced and preserved. And more important, the tribes that survived were those that listened with enough understanding to benefit from the skills of their members. And, of course, being listened to and being understood therefore contributed greatly to our belonging feelings, so that the two core needs, being understood and belonging, fed into each other.

Also from birth, built into us, we know that we need to master skills that are valuable to the tribe. Tribe members who are very good at important jobs are held in high esteem and given extra privileges. Masterful tribe members are seen as "right" more often, listened to more often, and given more attention.

We also know that tribe members who wanted to procreate chose a mate and that those with a mate had a strong helper and an extra "layer" of protection, and since most other members "mated," it was another way to "fit in." We also know something about status. We are prepared to learn very early how to recognize someone's position in the tribe. We very easily pick up on the nonverbal cues that convey status, the down-putting glances or the looking-up-to gazes, the shunning or the grace-bestowing gestures, the mild forms of aggressive one-upsmanship or the signals that we are viewed as equals. And there are the physical social status indicators, which evolution has also made us prepared to recognize. The strongest tribe members, those perceived as the most needed, usually have the best food and the best place to sleep or best nesting materials (the rich eat well in palatial houses on the hill). They receive the most attention and affection from tribe members, including the opposite sex, and they are first in line for extras and benefits. In Malcolm Gladwell's 2007 book *Blink*, the author cites research that shows taller people make more money than shorter people. This is clearly an indicator that our tribal signals are still in play.

More, More, More

Given this knowledge it is easy to assume that even someone who grew up in a healthy tribe where most of their basic needs were met, like most of us in Western societies, would still be motivated to "stay on top of things" by gathering more food and nesting materials, by trying to get the strongest, healthiest, most attractive mate available in the tribe, and by trying to maintain a high position within the tribe. In other words, it is absolutely human *nature* to be constantly seeking *more* of everything. Healthy individuals who get their basic needs met over time may have the luxury of keeping these primitive needs in check when they enter the self-actualization process. In later, more advanced stages of development, in other words, the importance of finding spiritual peace and serenity and of giving back to the world may enable such a developed person to move beyond simply seeking more of the basic survival-based needs. Gordon Gecko, the money- and power-hungry protagonist in Oliver Stone's film *Wall Street*, rationalizes his deeds with the statement, "Greed is good." While the "goodness" of greed can be argued, I would agree that greed, or what I label *More-seeking*, is certainly built into us.

Given that Belonging and Being Listened To are critical, core needs, a *healthy* individual who belongs to a healthy tribe experiences a *moderate* level of intensity of all other needs. Healthy individuals have some level of faith that their needs will be met, enabling them to exercise moderation in the More-seeking. Healthy individuals have also come to believe that they themselves have an impact on the outcomes they experience. They see the connections between their actions and what happens to them. They have learned to ask for things and to contribute to their own success.

The Revamped Hierarchy of Needs

The result of redesigning the hierarchy of needs, my view of how humans develop, is pictured in Figure 4.1. It incorporates the ordering of the sequence of needs, with physical safety before physiological needs, then after physiological needs, the need for psychological/emotional safety, followed by the esteem of others, self-esteem and finally self-actualization. Surrounding this entire pyramid-shaped hierarchy are the overriding, all-encompassing needs of, first, Belonging and Touch and then Being Understood and Listened To.

Figure 4.1
Healthy Development

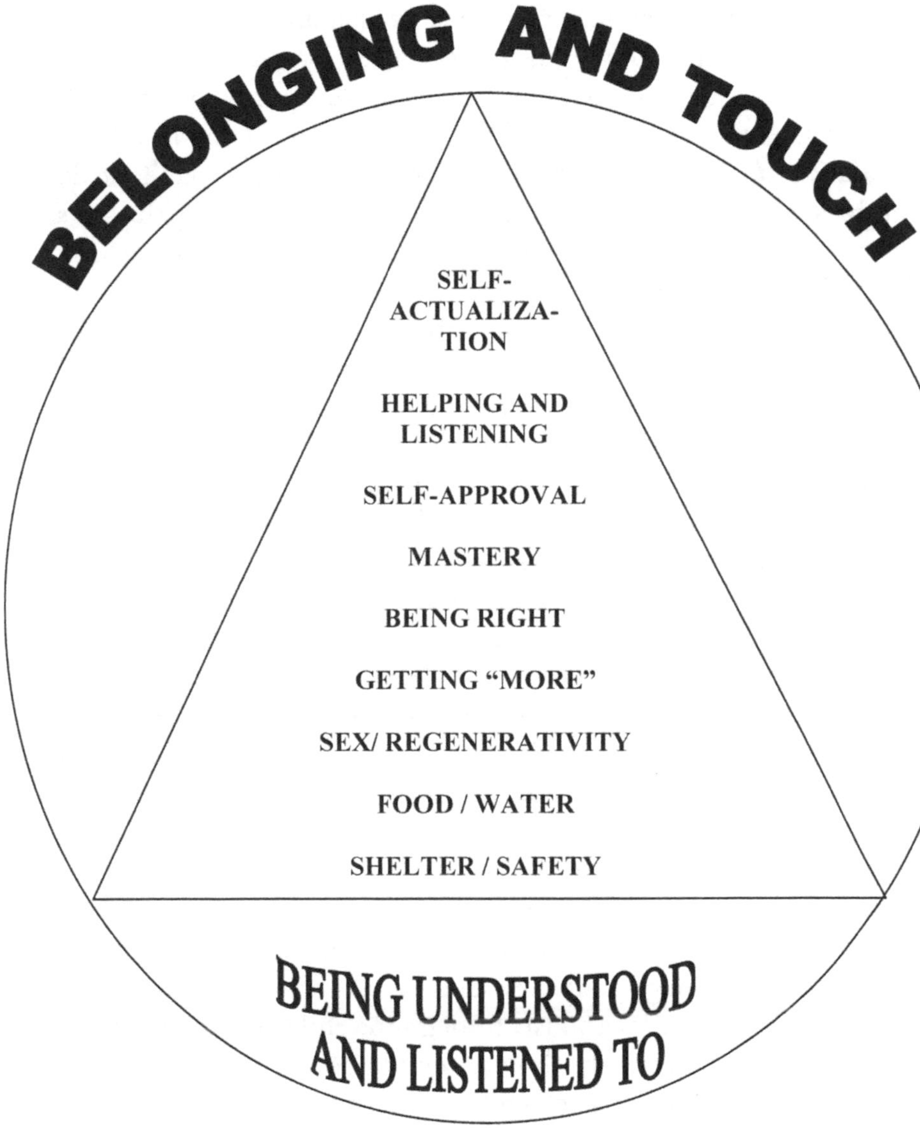

BELONGING AND TOUCH

SELF-
ACTUALIZA-
TION

HELPING AND
LISTENING

SELF-APPROVAL

MASTERY

BEING RIGHT

GETTING "MORE"

SEX/ REGENERATIVITY

FOOD / WATER

SHELTER / SAFETY

**BEING UNDERSTOOD
AND LISTENED TO**

The Results Of Unmet Basic Needs

Let us imagine what happens when the basic needs are not met. Someone who does not get enough food will have their most primitive strings plucked and will probably always want more of everything in order to feel safe from extinction. Someone who is not kept safe and protected may never believe that any neighborhood is safe. But when a person's needs to *belong* or *be listened to* are not met, almost any of the other needs can be affected, since all other needs are dependent on belonging and being listened to. If you lack food, or safety, *and* do not belong or are not listened to, then what hope do you have of alleviating your hunger or lack of safety? Hopelessness follows when something essential is lacking *and* there is no socially acceptable way of filling that lack.

Take a look at some of the ways the need for belonging can be expressed when it is not met, keeping in mind that having "a need not met" is subjective. This means that it does not matter whether others think the evaluation is true or not. An opinion like "How can he feel unsafe? He lives in one of the lowest crime communities in the nation!" is of no consequence. What does matter is whether the individual *believes/feels/experiences* (or does not) that his or her essential needs are satisfied. Attempting to amass vast amounts of money and possessions (our society's equivalent of great nesting materials and status in the tribe) is a likely sign that a person feels insecure about their position in the tribe. Seeking to be *Alpha*, or the most powerful person in the tribe, is the only way they can feel safe and secure. Mastering skills to excess in order to become the most valued resource person in the tribe one belongs to is potentially another way of expressing the belief that one does not securely belong. Excessive bragging can be a bid for status in whatever tribe the bragging is occurring. It is especially interesting to watch people who consistently brag about their children. At first it may seem that they are merely living vicariously through the children. It is, however, possible to live vicariously through children without fanfare. The bragging is a way of using the children as a bargaining chip to gain status in a group through association with a high status individual, their own accomplished child. This particular phenomenon gives insight into why people "hang" with famous individuals. Getting close to and being honored by Alpha is another way of gaining status in the tribe. This emulation-type behavior is adaptive in children, who are naturally watching and imitating the adults who they can see are already "in" and held in high regard by the tribe. But, as a person gets older and develops their own identity, this particular need can be transcended for more important desires. It often is not though. Another "quick fix" status elevator is a form of communication called triangulation, wherein two people unite to talk derisively about a third person or group of people. Those who are doing the triangulating feel a sense of camaraderie and connection. Exclusion of others by definition means that the persons who are not excluded, those doing the excluding, *belong* together. It is also a status elevator since someone else being put down elevates the down-putter and the co-conspirator, or "partner in crime." Unfortunately, these quick fixes do not last long and the cycle starts up again very soon. A person who feels a lack of belonging may also insist that they are right about everything, or consistently argue with almost everyone. These people seem to be almost screaming out to be understood.

Some very destructive, antisocial behaviors emerge when people feel unsatisfied in the mental and emotional places within them that house the basic needs. And this is especially true when the basic needs not met are the most essential – belonging and being listened to.

Core Drivers Of Behavior

Now is a good time to explore the reinforcements and punishers in life and how they work. Here is a universal truth that will help guide your goal-setting work and enable you to understand how others function. *Pain avoidance is the number one driver of behavior in the world.* People will usually abandon all other activities and even engage in self-destructive behaviors to avoid pain or the threat of pain. This is not to say that a person cannot overcome the need to avoid pain, and then choose to do something else. And in fact many times when people mindfully look at the whole picture, they take the painful immediate consequence to avoid some other more painful or "wrong" consequence. This is perhaps the case when a Secret Service agent steps in front of a bullet so his or her President does not take the bullet. Mother Teresa endured the pain of living among the poorest, most sickly of persons in Calcutta, apparently because she felt she would have experienced ignoring the plight of these people as more harrowing or more wrong than living among them. But when you see someone doing something that appears to be counterintuitive and that you know is destructive, look for what may be causing them pain elsewhere to make them go from the frying pan into the fire. For example, a grief stricken person who drinks to the point of physical deterioration to avoid the feelings of pain and loss is clearly so bent on avoiding one kind of pain that he or she does not notice, or care about, the other pain encroaching on him or her.

We need to realize that while pain avoidance is a strong motivator and people will often work very hard under threat of losing a job or a spouse, or to avoid disapproval from significant people, this type of motivator carries with it many side effects. People are shoved back to a place in the needs hierarchy that they find scary and uncomfortable, so they may become frustrated, angry and resentful, causing anything from simmering resentment to unnecessary conflict to overt vengeance. I often find myself warning managers and owners of businesses to stop aggressive, scary and sometimes shaming techniques to motivate employees. The threatened parties are in a constant state of fight or flight preparedness so they may suffer health issues and accidents due to distraction, costing themselves and their company much money. And if the pain gets too intense, they may even find another frying pan or fire to jump into. So, yes, sometimes it works to find a pain severe enough to get someone to work hard and work smart. But beware if you or someone you know is delivering or receiving such "cattle prod" motivation. It can be costly or deadly if not managed carefully.

A better, safer motivator is some incentive or reinforcer to work toward. I consistently ask people to tell others and to think in terms of what they want (e.g., "I want to be appreciated") rather than in terms of what they wish to avoid (e.g., "I wish he'd stop complaining"). The incentives must be tailored to the individual at his or her present stage of development. This is not only because one person's pleasure is another person's pain, but also because what once gave satisfaction earlier in one's life may now fail to do so. A simple example is that the value of spending time with Mom and Dad clearly changes over the eras of most people's lives. A more complex example is the safety a relatively undeveloped person may so strongly seek. The prospect of attaining that safety will not have the same power as a motivator once the safety-seeker has enough self-esteem and skills to provide him- or herself with safety. Even after we determine that a reward or punisher of behavior is, subjectively, a strengthener or punisher *for this person at this time in his or her life*, we still need to know if there is some subjective threat blocking the pursuit of the incentive. For example a person who believes that even reasonable safety is an illusion may not work hard for any amount of money if there is a need to go into what he considers an unsafe neighborhood to earn that money. A sales person who is afraid of flying will probably not try to win a sales contest when the winner gets a trip that involves flying.

Positive and Negative Drivers Of Behavior Interacting

In order to demonstrate what blocking of the pursuit of incentives can look like, and what forms pain avoidance can take, I tell a story to clients and seminar participants about a little boy at the bottom of the stairs in his house. He is standing at the bottom of the stairs looking up longingly because he knows that his favorite toy is in the room at the top. Unfortunately, he also "knows" that there is a monster at the top of the stairs, hiding just out of view. As he stands safely in the well-lighted living room at the bottom of the stairs, if he were to rate how much he wants the toy on a scale from 1 to 10 (1 being "hardly at all," and 10 being "more than anything in the world"), he might give his desire for the toy an 8. The fear would rate a 2 (1 being "none at all", 10 being "the most fear I have ever felt"). He breathes in deep and steps up to the second stair. He cautiously stops and listens. With some tentativeness, he steps up again. His body tightens a bit and his breath shortens. His fear is now a 4. Steeling himself again, he mounts the fourth step. Stopping again to listen, he holds his breath now, waiting. As he takes another step up, he stops short and thinks that he has heard the monster. He feels his body tighten and clenches his fists. He is sweating and breathing in short gasps. He does not know it, but his blood pressure is rising, his circulation is speeding up. His blood is being diverted from his organs and going to his large muscles, ready to fight or "to flight." All the boy knows is that he is scared and tight. As he forces himself up onto the sixth step, he freezes at the thought of catching a glimpse of the monster. His fear has risen to an 8 on the scale, equal to the desirability of the toy. The thought, "I can't go on" clinches the deal, and he turns to run down the stairs. As he races down, the fear diminishes. When he reaches the bottom he collapses with relief. The toy is the reinforcement incentive and the monster is the block to the goal. The decision to quit and the act of running away comprise the anesthetic, or pain reliever.

Now consider that, in addition to pain avoidance, *mastery is a natural human need*. Sometimes, however, to complicate things, there is a shaming parent at the bottom of the stairs to tell the boy that he is a coward. If this happens often enough, eventually a second "mind monster" materializes. Now the boy is between a rock and a hard place when he tries to traverse the stairs. He wants the toy, but the monster at the top is in the way. He wants to run to relieve this pain, but he also sees the monster at the bottom of the stairs, the shaming parent (or the shame itself, if the parent's shaming message has been internalized). At some point, in order to "save face," the boy will stay away from the stairs and start saying things like, "I never really liked that toy anyway." Or he will find some pain reliever like self-harm or seclusiveness to hide from all of the monsters. We all know people who had some difficulty "fitting in" and who at some point began acting like they did not want to fit in. In other words, sometimes people become so threatened by the monsters that they take "preemptive" strikes, such as rejecting others before others have the chance to reject them. So far, for the little boy on the stairs, the monsters have been "monsters in his mind." But after a while, the monsters in the mind chase people right into real monsters. When the "toy" for a company is an *untried target market* and the mind monster is the *fear of investing and getting no return*, the real monster is *diminishing profits due to stagnation*. Companies are all subject to "living" their owners' monsters. The Fourteenth Amendment may have made corporations "real people" for legal purposes, but it could not find a way for companies to free themselves from their owner's "monsters." If the mind monster for a newly hired executive is *fear of public speaking* (needing the approval of the tribe so much that the possibility of not getting it is terrifying) and the incentive or "toy" is the *paycheck*, the real monster is *not paying the bills and losing everything*. When this rock and hard place converge, self-destructive behavior in the form of using some other pain reliever, such as drugs or alcohol, becomes very likely. And then, of course, the person has just invited a whole new group of monsters into the game.

Navigating The Hierarchy Of Needs With Mindfulness

It is becoming clear that the reinforcers people will work for and the punishers they will work to avoid are universal. First, we all share the hierarchy of needs and, second, pain avoidance is the number one driver of all living creatures. These reinforcers and punishers are individual in their details because each of us is moving through, or is stuck at and failing to move through, a different section of the needs hierarchy and each of us has found that different behaviors and pain relievers work for us. Furthermore, some people make Herculean efforts, or simply excel in their abilities, to overcome basic needs and work for something of a higher order. A historical example is Ghandi. The man was willing to go hungry and to put himself in a position that he knew would entice assassins so that he could serve a higher purpose. But if like most of us, you are a "regular" person, then knowing the hierarchy of needs and understanding where you are on it will help you to determine what you are working for and what you are avoiding.

The only way to safely navigate and to set goals that will work for you is to be mindfully aware of places that you are stuck. Being mindfully aware is a simple principle, but can be difficult to maintain. It is, however, mostly about being honest with yourself and your closest support people. If you know that you come from a background of poverty where your needs were never adequately met, you can stay aware of a possible tendency to over-collect or to compete too aggressively for material things. If you know that being "right" is the driving force you have come to use to get attention and esteem, you can admit to your closest people that you have a tendency to argue just for the sake of arguing.

A Lot To Be Mindful Of

I would like to re-visit the eating and healthy lifestyle topic with which I started this chapter. We established that the hows are covered, written and spoken about with extreme repetition, and that most people have all of the information they need in order to set goals of living a life filled with healthy eating and exercise. Now that we know that it is the whys and not the hows that will make the difference, what is left to say about why so many people do not live the healthy lifestyle? Obviously, they are finding other things that have greater incentive value, and/or there are "monsters" blocking their way to the incentives.

Food is the first pain killer we ever encounter. For evidence of this, just look back at our development. Hunger to an infant *is* pain. Since food alleviates the hunger, it kills the pain. A healthy person may never use food to anesthetize other types of pain, but a person who has their very survival threatened by not feeling that they belong may turn to this most familiar pain killer. "Since it worked for physical pain," they think wishfully, at some level of awareness, "maybe it will work for emotional pain and fear." And it does! At least for a short time it works. Then the pain returns and the cycle begins again. There are even types of foods that prove to be especially enticing since they create biological changes that are emotionally "helpful." Unfortunately most of these "helpfully" comforting foods contain excessive amounts of sugar and fat. Even after delving deeply into the belonging issues that originally caused the eating problems, many people find that the eating addiction remains difficult to tackle. There are several sensible and logical reasons for this. First, we cannot avoid food. And unhealthy, tempting foods are far more likely to be encountered than healthy ones. There is also the fact that eating to excess is built in. We are prepared to eat as much as we can when we encounter food because our "cave person" is telling us that we do not know when the next meal will be. Think about it. Have you ever seen a lion stop eating and say, "I have had enough gazelle for now, I'm full. Why don't you have some?" Finally, food has incredible power as an *immediate* pleasure giver; even before it can be metabolized, the very eating of chocolate or other comfort food makes us feel better. Even subhuman animals love sweets. Dairy cattle produce more milk when fed the outdated candy that the farms buy up from candy stores. That is a very strong motivator. As compared to the quickness of the fix, the benefits of controlling our intake of food are very far off.

I want to stress the point here, though, that, just like all other behaviors, the unhealthy lifestyle behaviors are planned. They may not be the result of mindful strategic planning, but nobody behaves without making a decision to behave unless they are severely disabled. If you did it, you planned it. If you said you were going to the fridge to get broccoli and you returned with chocolate cake, somewhere between what you said and what you did, you changed the plan. As we will see in the next chapter, this is the reason that making mindful, written goals is so important. With goals set mindfully and then documented, it is much more difficult to fool yourself into believing that you were somehow taken over or that you accidentally engaged in "bad" behavior.

Where We Must Begin To Lead A Goal-Directed Life

The first step in goal-setting is to understand **why** we will, or will not, strive for and reach a goal. Rooted in our biology as animals descended most recently from cave people, we possess the well-understood needs for sustenance, shelter and safety. In addition, we humans display the more advanced need to be esteemed by important others in our lives, and to possess esteem we maintain within ourselves, that is, self-esteem. Finally, given solid foundations and opportunities to flourish during our development, we have within us, and can come to be motivated by, a highly advanced need to fulfill our true selves and give back to our community; this is the need for self-actualization. What is clear also is that there are two needs closest to the core of us, the need to belong and the related need to be understood and listened to. These needs are all-important, since they underlie and make possible the satisfaction of all other needs. Many of our failures to reach or even set goals, and our repetition of old patterns that leave no room for reaching new goals, are due to failure to have other, more basic needs met. In addition, we often fail to reach our goals because we are wrapped up in the most common driver of behavior, the avoidance of pain. Over-involvement in pain avoidance blocks goal-setting and goal-getting by letting fear or shame, the most common pains we avoid, dictate most of our actions. This drains our energy away from goal-focused actions and away from the achievement of mastery of new, self-advancing skills and attitudes. Only highly vigilant mindfulness – watching our thoughts, perceptions, and actions with honesty and openness – gives us any chance of even setting realistic goals, let alone reaching them.

Chapter 5

Ready, Set, Goal: Goal-Setting Part 2

You now know how important the whys are to goals
So don't trouble yourself trying to find the loopholes.
But the hows can come now that you have that straight.
Why don't you get to work and don't procrastinate.

When it comes to setting goals that will make you able,
The tool of choice is the Decisional Balance Table.
Use it each and every time you take aim at a goal,
So you can set out on the course with heart and soul.

The decisions that you make will all have pros and cons,
But all you need is this tool and working neurons.
Make sure you know the monsters that are heading your way,
And don't forget the toys with which you want to play.

Here are all the facts about how change takes place,
So you end up where you want and not in outer space.
You won't get far if you can't delay gratification.
Be sure to take in *that* vital information.

You may be able to begin by running from the stick,
But having carrots up ahead will get you through the thick.
There may be payoffs and urges to stay right where you be
And prices to pay when you reach that goal you see.

When you can be sure of a mastery orientation,
Set your dial and tune to the change station.
Take the time to remain in your mindful mode,
And decisions will be smoother at the crossroad.

The Plain White Rapper

In business, many times when a decision needs to be made, the leadership engages in a process called "cost-benefit analysis." It is exactly as it sounds. The responsible parties calculate what doing something will cost and what the benefits of that something are. For example, if a retail store is planning to eliminate their shoe department, they may list the benefits as more space and employee time to sell something else and more focus on other items. The potential costs may be fewer customers and possible loss in sales. They would of course include exact dollar amounts where they had them and calculate or estimate others where needed.

I believe the process of cost-benefit analysis (CBA) works in businesses, in Me, Inc and in We, Inc for simple behaviors, such as whether or not to engage in a specific activity. For example, one of my twins loves to argue (he has already decided to become an attorney). Through numerous discussions about the costs to our relationship and my stress level of arguing every little point, and the benefits, or what he is likely to gain, I now need only to say, "Do a CBA on that" for him to stop and make a determination of whether he should continue to argue his point. For larger, more complicated decisions and important instances of Goal Setting, the field of Psychology has given us the Decisional Balance Table, an expanded CBA, or a CBA-zilla, pictured in Figure 5.1.

The idea of Decisional Balance is based on the research and thinking of James Prochaska, John Norcross and Carlo DiClemente as expressed in their book, *Changing for Good*. Put simply, Decisional Balance is the examination of the pros and cons, the rewards and the prices to be paid, of making a change in your life or not making that change. This examination is worth doing, in fact essential to do, to give change efforts their best chance of succeeding *or* to make an informed, intelligent decision not to attempt a change. The

Decisional Balance Table summarizes our personal whys at the time we are contemplating a change. It does so in a useful way that tells us whether the whys, our present motives to change, are adequate to enable us to proceed to the hows. The Decisional Balance method bridges the whys to the hows.

Foundations Of The Decisional Balance Approach

The Decisional Balance Table in Figure 5.1 is based on some assumptions.

1. Change is a process, not an event. Some small to medium changes may be event-like. There is probably not a detailed process involved in my deciding to go from formal suits to "business casual" in my style of dress. But even changes like this may involve a somewhat complex pre-change process, with such questions as, "How will my peers accept the change?" and "Will my style of dress affect how I relate to people, or my fundamental sense of who I am?" An honest confronting of the issues and questions raised in the *process* of a well-done Decisional Balance evaluation will make clear the process nature of change and in fact give a taste of doing a process.

2. Soul-searching and sometimes painful honesty will set the stage for and promote good change. So rationalizations and excuses are best left at the door for the Decisional Balance process.

3. Fear or dislike of the negative consequences of current behavior may be enough drive to *begin* a change process, but experiencing the plusses and payoffs of the new, changed behavior is the factor that will motivate a person to *complete and maintain* the change. Facing financial crisis, no time with the family, or a bleak retirement may start a move toward a new, more lucrative career choice. But experiencing the greater wealth and, probably more importantly, the freedom and stimulation of the new work, will keep the changer on the new course. Fear only drives

people so far, then positive consequences and rewards are necessary.

4. Every change, however good it looks or in fact is, carries with it costs and new challenges. The promotion or the move to an upscale neighborhood, bestowing heftier pay, greater recognition and prestige and heightened creature comfort, also carries new, loftier work and production expectations, social pressures, and many of the same difficult kinds of people as you encountered in the former position or neighborhood.

5. Backsliding, mistaken judgments (wrong choices at forks in the road), lapses, relapses and sometimes outright collapses of the change process are much more the rule than the exception. Seldom are change processes undertaken that move in a nearly straight, upward-sloping path to glorious fruition. This is why we have so many catchphrases to describe imperfect change: "course correction," "Plan B" and "learning from our mistakes" are three common ones. Working in the Decisional Balance model invites us to look thoughtfully at those factors that are likely to precipitate deviations from the ideal path of change. With the resulting knowledge, we can probably lower the chances of destructive degrees of deviation, or at least make plans for how to deal with them. Think about driving a car. Mindful, "hands on the wheel," constant tiny corrections are what keep the car moving in the proper direction. And even when mindlessness and/or carelessness make dramatic corrections necessary, we make them and go on.

6. Change needs support to succeed. "None of us is as smart as all of us." Pooled intellect always surpasses the intellect of even the brightest of us. Minimally, people will need emotional support, especially when those almost inevitable lapses or junctions of doubt present themselves. And beyond, but not more

important than emotional support, most changes require material support. In some cases, support in the forms of money, time and physical effort will be obvious needs. Less obviously, changes occur not only as processes but also within social networks. Therefore, the support of cooperation and coordination with significant other parties is often critical to successful change. If one member of a couple who has been submissive and unassertive is to have much chance of becoming more assertive, at least within that relationship, the other partner will need to become less aggressive, a better listener and more willing to take direction from the partner seeking to find his or her voice.

The Decisional Balance Tool

The Decisional Balance Table in Figure 5.1 explains each of the four quadrants.

Figure 5.1
Decisional Balance Table Explanation

	PROS	**CONS**

THE CHANGED STATE	**A. Payoffs for New Behavior**
	
	Benefits to be gained from the change
	Things to look forward to through changing
	The vision of the future
	
	MASTERY-ORIENTED
		B. Challenges Caused by New Behavior
		
		Anticipated difficulties to be faced
		Problems that may arise
		Feelings that may come up
		   that cause discomfort or pain
		Tolerance of feelings may be an issue
		This is the "feel and deal" box:
		   identify problem feelings
		   and how to deal with them
		May be Monsters in the Mind
		
		AVERSION-AVOIDANT

THE UNCHANGED STATE	**C. Payoffs for Present Behavior**
	
	Primary and secondary gains
	   of the current state
	What you are "getting out of it"
	Can be dark side work: Identifying
	   and owning up to those feelings
	   or thoughts we do not want to
	   have or do not want to admit we have
		D. Negative Consequences of Present Behavior
		
		What you are dealing with now
		   in the present state
		The disadvantages of the
		   current behaviors
		May be Real Monsters

A Critical Ability

Before we begin to work with this tool, let us define mastery-oriented versus aversion avoidant people by looking at a classic study begun in the 1960s by Walter Mischel on delay of gratification in children. In this study, four-year olds were taken into a room where there was a marshmallow on a table. They were offered the opportunity to receive two marshmallows, if they waited for the examiner to return from a supposed errand without eating the single marshmallow. The examiner left the room for about fifteen to twenty minutes, which is an eternity for a small child. If the child did not wait, they only got the one marshmallow. Approximately two-thirds of the children waited and became known as the

"Delayers." They used self-distraction, such as talking to themselves, singing and covering their eyes to suffer the wait. The one-third who did not wait, known as the "Grabbers," typically pounced on the marshmallow within seconds of the examiner's exit. About fourteen years later, when the researchers followed up on these children, the Delayers were doing better academically than the Grabbers. They were also more socially well-adjusted, less likely to be engaged in delinquent behaviors and fighting, and had higher SAT scores. They handled pressures without coming undone, embraced challenges and persisted in the face of difficulties, were self-reliant, confident, trustworthy, dependable and initiative-taking. The Grabbers, on the other hand, were seen as shying away from social contacts, as stubborn and indecisive, as easily frustrated, as immobilized by stress and as managing emotions poorly, generally with fighting or arguing. Their self-esteem was clearly affected as well. While this research did not study other characteristics or the home lives of the children, those of us with clinical skills and years of experience with clients can make some logical extrapolations. It is likely that the Grabbers had inadequate faith in themselves and in the system in which they were living. It is likely that the Grabbers believed either that the second marshmallow would not be forthcoming and/or that they did not have the capability to wait without horrendous consequences. They probably particularly believed that they were incapable of tolerating pain and suffering.

When talking about making changes and achieving goals, I refer to people who would be Delayers as Mastery-Oriented and people who would be Grabbers as Aversion-Avoidant. With Grabbers, as with the boy on the stairs in the last chapter, the fear of potential pain, the belief that he/she cannot handle it, and the sheer "unknownness" of what else is at the top of the stairs, are scary enough to make the toy up there (the "second marshmallow") fade from awareness and consideration.

As we begin to use the Decisional Balance tool, it becomes clear that the ability to delay gratification, or impulse control, and the ability to keep our eye on a longer-range prize, are critical in achieving or even having the courage to set goals. To help you fill in the cells of the table, refer to your SWOT analysis. Many of your goals originated here, and the SWOT analysis results can provide a broad perspective which can help keep your impulses controlled, your gratification adequately delayed, and your sights on the larger, longer-range prize.

For More Than One-time Use

The beauty of the Decisional Balance Table as a tool is that it can be used throughout the change process. Box A, the Pros of the Changed State, in which the new behavior will be occurring, is the box that shows the "vision of the future." Here, we write those incentives and positive consequences that we would like to attain and experience, and *especially those we can realistically foresee*. Here we make prominent in our awareness all the reinforcements, or "toys at the top of the stairs," that we can see coming our way when we successfully make the changes. For mastery-oriented people, this is the most important box. Box D is the opposite of Box A. Here we write the Cons of the Unchanged State, all of the negative effects of the current behaviors, the missing or lost "toys", the low self-esteem, the tarnished or absent relationships, everything from lost money to lost freedom. These are often the real monsters, such as high blood pressure and cholesterol for someone whose current state is poor dietary habits. With some changes though, these are just issues that need to be addressed. For example, when deciding on moving to a new house or to a new job, this box may just contain the important faults of the current house or job. Boxes A and D really should be considered together. This is in part because of the third assumption above, that Box D, the current "bad stuff," may motivate the beginning of change, but looking ahead to and then experiencing Box A, the future "good stuff," will keep the change going. Exploration of Boxes A and D should also be done in tandem because sometimes Box D may be filled with really awful, discouraging, demoralizing items. Looking only at these might lead the would-be changer to become hopeless and quit before ever beginning.

Box B is the Cons of the Changed Behavior. For the little boy on the stairs, this would be "having to fight the monster." For people of all ages, however, approaching the fear and especially succeeding at handling the fear may be creating expectations that may then raise the bar for the future. Many people shy away from otherwise good changes, like promotions, because they believe that "more and more will be expected of me." This box often contains the "mind monsters." We call this box the "feel and deal" box because sometimes it involves admitting that we have fears and then finding ways to face these fears. For example, if I fear that in my new, promoted position, demands will just increase endlessly, then I will need to have or develop the assertiveness to set limits, delegate work, and to say "no."

Finally, Box C contains the Pros of the Unchanged State. These are the reinforcements, or "payoffs," of the current behaviors. For the boy on the stairs, this box would contain the anxiety relief he feels once he quits and runs, the absolution from the responsibility to do anything constructive, and possibly other "good" things depending on what he or others do when he arrives at the bottom of the stairs. A comforting dish of ice cream from Mom, or consolation from well-meaning but overly sympathetic friends, may further reinforce the avoidance behavior. The contents of Box C are often difficult to confront honestly. Completed honestly, this box often contains those payoffs of our current behavior that we do not want to admit. For example, a bully who has been saying that he just "can't control" his temper will need to admit that one of the strongest motives for his bullying is that those he bullies cower, shut up, give him his own way, and overall make him feel powerful.

Being Honest About Payoffs

When completed with total honesty, the Decisional Balance Table gives one a very clear picture of the "monsters in the mind," the "real monsters" and all of the payoffs. It also makes it obvious that just as in a business, individuals only do what they are being paid to do. Payments can come in many different positive forms: money, food, attention, pity, touch and/or sex, pats on the back and kudos, self-esteem or the esteem of others, bragging rights, the envy of other people, "touchdown dances," and so on. And of course there are various forms of that hugest of behavior drivers, the avoidance and reduction of pain. While we know that the basic reinforcers are universal, the potency of any one reinforcer, punisher or "pain reliever" is completely subjective. Only the individual person and his or her subjective experience determine where a reinforcer is on the hierarchy of power to influence behavior, and this power to influence can change over time. The good news is that *you do* know what is true *for you*, what incentives and rewards you will perform work to get, *at any given time*. You may be hiding it from yourself or denying the knowledge, but with thoughtfulness and/or help from a support system, you will be able to fill the sections of the Decisional Balance table for any of your issues.

In Figure 5.2 there is an example of a completed Decisional Balance Table, for someone who has an anger or temper issue. The contents of Box B and especially of Box C illustrate some of the negative thoughts and psychological facts one may need to face to do a truly fearless and searching Decisional Balance analysis. It is not for the faint of heart or those without adequate faith in the process or in the usefulness of available, caring support people.

Figure 5.2
Decisional Balance Table, Temper Example

	PROS	CONS

STABLE, EVEN TEMPER	**A. Payoffs of New Behavior**
	
	Approach, closeness to others
	More secure that others will stay
	Peace of mind
	Feeling in control of self
	Better health
	Respect of spouse and self and children
	Increased productivity
	No shame in daily life
	Sense of accomplishment
		B. Challenges of New Behavior
		
		Loss of control of others
		Having to live with feelings of
		  loneliness, inadequacy,
		  and fear and threat
		Much effort to learn new ways to
		  cope with feelings
		Uncertainty because all important
		  relationships will change
		Need to talk and confess acts
		  that are considered "bad"

SHORT, ERRATIC TEMPER	**C. Payoffs of Present Behavior**
	
	Control by intimidation.
	Attached to "winning"
	  and getting my own way
	Sense of "righteousness,"
	  feeling anger is "justifiable"
	Can just avoid talk about bad behaviors
	  and forget them
	Outbursts relieve physical symptoms
	  of rage
	Rage avoids other feelings
		D. Consequences of Present Behavior
		
		Alienation by loved ones and others
		High blood pressure
		Cycles of rage then loneliness
		  and regret
		Constant unsettled feeling
		Loss of respect and likeability
		Constant apologies or
		  justifications needed
		Shame and failure feelings

When consulting in a business, it is sometimes difficult to teach the idea that anything anyone is doing, they are being "paid" to do. The payment controls the behavior. If you control the payment, then you control the behavior. Sometimes the payment is literally money, such as when a supervisor says, "She gets on the Internet and shops, and doesn't look up to see there is a customer at the counter." Obviously, the employee is being paid to sit and do what she is doing – she is collecting her paycheck. And obviously there is no "real monster" sharpening its claws in the background. So, my advice to the supervisor is, "Go in the back room and make a monster. Then come out and show it to the employee." This combined with making sure that there are "perks" for excellent customer service could take the employee to a mastery-orientation quickly. This is when the "whys" of goal setting become very transparent. Often, we hear something like, "But that's a lot of work. We would have to monitor the computer time and watch too closely." Or, worse, we hear, "I don't want to hurt her feelings," or "She will just hate me then." That is the Emperor saying, "I want everyone to say that I am dressed, but going and getting clothes on is too much trouble." Solutions are hard work, especially when a destructive behavior has been allowed to go on and on and become strong enough to be a bad habit. We often ask for a solution when we do not really want a solution. It is okay to just want to "vent" occasionally, as long as you do not make a lifetime habit out of it, you are honest about what you are doing and you are doing it with someone who will not help you turn it into triangulation.

What about your Me, Inc or your We, Inc? The same rules need to apply. If your direct reports, your children, are engaging in behaviors that you do not like, you are probably paying them to do these behaviors. Just check the system. Are there any situations where your children behave in the desired way? There are probably certain rules in your family that are "non-negotiable." Look at the reinforcers and the punishers surrounding these rules. Then look at the system surrounding those behaviors that you "can't stand" but that are going on anyway. Chances are the person who delivers the payoffs is slacking off and causing the system not to work. In cases like this, the hows of behavior management are working fine. The whys are failing. Rats and dogs and even turtles respond to behavior modification, so certainly the people will. It is almost certain that if the company leader is "doing it right," the employees will follow. If the leader, or parent, is concerned about being liked instead of respected, or if the supervisor is trying to be friends with the employees instead of being a great leader, or if the leader would prefer to lecture, yell or complain when things go wrong rather than exert the effort to put a good system in place, then the leader needs some coaching. When I am consulting with a business owner or manager and I keep hearing "Yes, but" to all of the solutions that are proposed, I know that I am dealing with an "Emperor." Usually the solution to this "roadblock" is to talk about the real monsters. In other words, ask, "What is going to happen if things stay the same?" Encourage yourself to think all of your strategies through. If at the end you meet up with a real monster, you may (or may not) be *stating* the right goals, but you are probably playing out and *living* the wrong goals.

To Proceed Or Not To Proceed With Change

When complete, the Decisional Balance Table can give you information of where you are in the change process. A "green light" Decisional Balance result is one in which Boxes A and D, and especially Box A, outweigh B and C. Remember that if Box D is full of negatives about the present state, but Box A has few perceived rewards for changing, the change could stall. You may choose to, or need to, start the change using the energy of Box D, avoiding aversion, but be looking for and be open to experiencing the rewards of the changed behavior, so that Box A, mastery-orientation, starts to fill.

There are some clear signs that it may be the wrong time or you may be in the wrong state of mind to begin a change. For example, if you cannot think of anything for Box A, but Box C is full, then you see no advantages to the change in question and can only see advantages to staying where you are. Successfully carrying out a change under these circumstances is very unlikely. Any completed Decisional Balance Table that has many items, or very difficult-to-surmount items, in Boxes B and C, is flashing a yellow caution light about proceeding with the change.

If, however, the Decisional Balance Table looks good, there is a positive vision of what the change will hold, and you can clearly see all the disadvantages of staying where you are, then it is time to look at the hows of changing. My seminar participants and clients get a little tip to help them use the Decisional Balance Table to its max, especially for those hard to change habits. It is a spin-off on what they teach in 12-step programs, the idea of "thinking the behavior through." For example, when an alcoholic wants a drink, he should consider not just what the next moment will be like, but what will happen when he has the second and the third, right up until the car crash or the black out or the fight, and so on. So what I recommend is that you take the worst items in Box D and "morph" them into an ugly "real" monster with teeth and keep it just behind you while you make the changes in your life. Try to spend most of the time focusing on the positives, but if at any time you think about quitting the change process, look back at those sharp teeth.

Mindfulness

As we have seen, and as makes good, common sense, everyone is living goals. The difference is that some people are willing to set mindful, conscious goals. Some people, those I called Bleacher Sitters in Chapter 2, are too afraid to actually articulate and commit to goals. They just keep making excuses because they are being driven by the monsters in their minds. These monsters may be fear of failure, fear of criticism, fear of not knowing what will happen next, or fear of being in the same room with their own feelings. Successful goal-setting, however, depends on our recognition of all of our monsters, so the first step to goal-setting and achievement is to be mindful. There are so many ways to become mindful. There are wonderful books on the subject, for example, *Stopping* by David Kundtz, *Wherever You Go, There You Are*, by Jon Kabat-Zinn, and *Breathe, You Are Alive* by Thich Nhat Hanh. The main theme is to be able to be aware of yourself and your environment as much of the time as possible. Just to show how "mindless" we are some of the time, think about the last time you drove somewhere and thought, "I don't remember getting here." Or recall the last time you misplaced something, knowing, "I just had the thing in my hand two minutes ago!" Driving around mindlessly in a ton or more of metal moving at high speeds is quite scary. And the object you have just mindlessly put down may be quite valuable. Many businesses work on teaching their employees mindfulness to reduce industrial accidents and to improve the output quality. It is the reason that lifeguards at conscientiously run public pools have to change posts every fifteen minutes, so that mindlessness from boredom or habituation does not set in.

Mindfulness as it relates to goals involves being able to ask yourself regularly, "Where have I been, where am I now, and where am I going?" You need to be able to answer these questions honestly *and* to be able at any time to answer, "What do I *really* want?" Businesses that I work with have retreats for the owners and managers so they can "breathe" and set their goals. Individuals, couples and families need retreats also to set the goals for their life businesses.

Getting To The Details

Goals can start out general and nebulous as they first take form in our minds. But they must become specific very soon. We start to create the masterpiece in our minds first, imagining the steps and the final product. Now is the time to write down the goals. Research has shown repeatedly that people who write goals down are much more likely to achieve them than people who just think them. It is also the time to get real specific. Goals need to be behavioral and measurable. In a business, the employee handbook would not say, "Be a good employee." It would instead define what a good employee does in behavioral terms. The less ambiguous, the more likely the business and the employee are to be happy and productive. You would not (unless you were my grandmother) say to put "part of a cup of milk" in a recipe. So, with your goals, be specific and measurable.

Check each goal step and understand that when you say "yes" to one thing, you are saying "no" to another. A business cannot produce everything or make their target market all people. When they try, they fail. When you say "yes" to mega-achievement goals, you are probably saying "no" to your family at least for a time. Sometimes there are creative ways to combine goals. For example, when you find ways to make more money per hour, there are more hours to spend on other things such as your family or hobbies. If you want to have lunch with two different people on the same day, you can have lunch with one and dinner with the other, or you can have lunch with both together.

Just be careful that you do not fool yourself into thinking that you can "have it all." Be realistic about what you really want and about how much of you there is available. It brings us back to the Emperor issue. I always tell people in my seminars that "You cannot have Life A and Consequences B." You get the end result of the goal steps to which you said "yes."

Make sure also that you like and will carry out the steps to the goals you wish to achieve. If you only like the end result of a goal, you will never get there. We all must do some things that we do not like to do, but it is unlikely that anyone will make a life of doing steps they hate just to get to an end. Life then becomes like spending eight hours a day at a job you dislike just for the paycheck. Few of us will do this, or if we do, the costs to our emotional health can be steep.

When you write the steps for your goals, do what sales people call "reverse engineering." Imagine that a sales person needs to sell ten alarm systems a week. If she knows from her past record that about 1 in 3 people who agree to see her face-to-face will buy, then she needs to pave the way to 30 face-to-face appointments per week. She will then need to calculate how many "cold calls" it takes to get those appointments. Hopefully she has kept careful records on the ratio of face-to-faces to cold calls, so she knows how many calls it takes to get the right number of "live" people on the telephone line. Then, finally, she will need to divide those calls into the number of days and hours she has to do the calling. She of course will need to allow the time for the face-to-face appointments when figuring when to fit in the call time. Just take your goal and back up a step at a time until you get to the smallest behavior that contributes to reaching the goal.

A family, or We, Inc example of this might be a mother who wants her family to be happy about and satisfied with family retreat weekends aimed at communing together and expressing feelings, wants, aspirations, and plans. In order to measure success, she has devised a satisfaction scale that includes not only productivity measures but items that measure feelings about the event. So, with reverse engineering in mind, she knows that everyone will need to "take time off" for some future long weekend. In order for everyone to participate willingly, they will need to see the value of such retreats. In order to see the value of a retreat, each family member will need to experience what it feels like to express themselves and for their feelings and opinions to matter. In order for this experience with self-expression to take place, the mother will need to take time each day to ask each family member to express their feelings and opinions and to make sure that the whole family is present for these moments. She will need to record her attempts with each family member and their responses. Therefore, the first step is to make sure that the family meets at least once a day, possibly over a meal, to have these special moments.

Make sure that each step is a measurable, observable, countable behavior. Do not set goals or have steps to those goals that are nebulous or you will never know if you did the steps or met the goal. Of course this translates as well to giving other people goals or jobs. In a business, the Human Resources department writes job descriptions and then the company provides training, management and coaching. In We, Inc, make sure that each member of the business or family has behavioral job descriptions. You cannot tell a child to "do the dishes." You must verbally describe and model the task, and then manage and coach their practice before the task can be accomplished. Reverse engineering, or what the psychological world calls backward chaining, can be an effective way of teaching a complicated behavior. For example, if you wanted to teach a child how to build a bicycle, you would start by assembling the entire bike, except for the last step or two. The child would complete the last steps and then the next time the step before plus the last steps, and so forth. This process would continue until the child was able to assemble the entire bike. Yes, it is a long process, but the lessons really "stick" and in the end you have a good employee/partner/child who gives a good satisfaction rating to his or her experience with the company.

Being On the Same Page and The Right Page

You already know from your SWOT analysis what your true calling is and what you are talented at. So you will only be looking to attain goals that are realistic for you. You also know from the SWOT analysis where your strengths lie, where you need help and what has already been done for you. For example, if you are putting together a recipe, some things need to be done from scratch, while others are already done very well by someone else who has boxed or bottled the item for you. An accountant who also knows computer programming would probably not want to take time away from earning money writing software to do word processing. That is a wheel that does not need re-inventing. Sometimes we need new wheels, such as rubber versus wood when we moved from buggy to automobile, but much of the time, someone else has already done it for us. Be reasonable and avoid the urge to "put your mark" on everything. There came a time when even "hard core" home bakers started to use boxed cake mixes because the manufacturers began doing such a good job of boxing ingredients that combined to make a great cake. Think before you "make it from scratch" so you do not use up your valuable time.

When businesses write their goals, they must compare the goals of each department and make certain that all departments are living the same *mission*, which is the answer to the question, "Why do we exist?" They must also make sure that each department is living the same *vision*, which is the answer to "Where do we want to go?" Departments must not be "at odds" with each other. It would be nothing short of self-destructive for the Sales department of a company to plan a huge marketing campaign for the U.S. while the Production department is producing Chinese instructions and metric system specifications for the product. All aspects of the Me, Inc business must "mesh" as well. Therefore, goals must be listed for each of your life's roles. You may be a partner, a parent, a friend, a community leader, a professional, and a church member. And keep in mind that all businesses need Housekeeping or Janitorial and Repair/Maintenance departments. These departments may be very small, but the goals and chores of these departments must be considered in the whole picture. Each of your roles must be in harmony with your life mission. If you have not written a mission statement for Me, Inc or for We, Inc, plan a retreat to do each of these tasks. When a business does not know why it exists, it will tend to go in random directions. Find out what your true calling is, or where your greatest love meets the world's greatest need. Write it down and keep it in a place where you can see it every day.

Putting The Right Jobs In The Right Hands

If at the end of your goal setting process, there are not enough hours in the day to do each of the steps, then there are some options.

Maybe you are trying to be the worker bee in too many departments of Me, Inc. Do a cost-benefit analysis on each of the departments and tasks, making sure to include your strengths and your own desires and emotions. If a company made the best cookware in the world, but had nobody to clean up the mess created by the production of the cookware, they would not shut the line down and have the production crew clean. The cost of shutting down would be far greater than hiring a janitor or two. If the designer of the cookware has a couple of hours free each week, it would certainly be unwise to assign her to "clean up" duty to save a few dollars on janitorial services. The "de-motivation" and insult to the designer who loves the one job for which she contracted could be way too costly, even if it looked on the surface as if she could put on a different hat for a while. You might reach a different conclusion if when the clean-up problem became clear, the designer had jumped up and said, "Oh, I love cleaning!" But even then, you would need to weigh the costs and benefits of having her versus someone else do the job.

Remember a cost-benefit analysis must take into account all variables. But when you do, you may feel overwhelmed by all the factors to consider. *You cannot run everything!* One of the lessons business owners need to learn early on is that if they insist on being in total control of everything, then they will probably not make much money. Delegating is necessary for any business to function. Even sole proprietorships that have no official employees hire out some of the jobs to consultants. They would not buy printing equipment when they need brochures published. In fact, some businesses exist solely to provide "departments" to other businesses. There are payroll companies, human resource outsourcing companies, free lance accountants, and janitorial companies. Life businesses need to hire out departments also. If you need to control every aspect of your life, then you will probably start to run out of steam and you will miss many opportunities. In a business, when employees are asked to work way too many hours or when they never feel "done" with anything, they experience very low job satisfaction. Some forms of downsizing become "dumbsizing." This is true when reductions in workforce are so severe or poorly thought out that the employees remaining after the cuts are oppressed by unwieldy workloads and/

or they must work in areas far removed from the skills for which they were hired.

You too will find life less than satisfying if you are everything to everybody in your life business. That is why it is necessary to "drill down" when considering what you need to keep doing and what you need to delegate. "Drilling down" here means looking at more than just the surface or obvious factors. Many times it will look as if you are saving money or gaining efficiency, when in fact the cost to your passion or even just your time is much greater than whatever is gained. A small, down-home example is morning coffee. A strict "bookkeeper" would probably say that home-brewed coffee costs only a few cents a day while the local drive-through costs a couple of dollars. Yes, in pure money the cost of the drive-through is greater. But what if the one-a-day, cherished cup of coffee is a real "starter" to a person who truly loves that local shop or the taste of their coffee? And what if the time spent making the coffee cuts into that precious ten minutes of personal connection time spent waking the kids in the morning? Cost-benefit analysis must take into account money and time, but also needs, energy and feelings. It is true that all of us have to "suck it up" sometimes and do jobs or make sacrifices that we do not want to do or make. Sometimes it turns out that the cost of not doing those jobs or making those sacrifices is too high. But when at all possible, make sure that you are spending the bulk of your time doing what you *love* to do.

With that point in mind, check out the *steps* to each of your goals and make sure that most of those steps, as well as the goals themselves, are lovable. Some can be just likeable and a very few can be merely tolerable. Beware though if the ratio of tolerable to lovable gets too great or if you have more than a very few that are "absolutely intolerable if I had to do this forever." Your life satisfaction may go too low. Just as employees who "hate work" are at risk for accidents, health problems and quitting, some people have bad physical reactions or engage in unsafe and unhealthy behaviors when their mind wants to escape their own Me, Inc or We, Inc. Some people even do escape their life business by thinking that running to another life business will solve the problem. Once in a while this works, but be very cautious about knowing what the problem really is. And remember, "Wherever you go, there you are." A change of scenery or of life partners will probably not heal longstanding, deep-seated dissatisfaction. Before you make a drastic move, you can check all of your p's and q's, but most important, check out those "whys" again. Why is your life unsatisfying? Is it really your life business or is it the person you have become? Is there a business partner that is dragging you down? Why do you not like the steps to the goals? Do you need to change your goals? Are you living someone else's goals? Did you choose one or more goals for the wrong reason? And, being deeply real with yourself, ask "Will I just make the same decisions again that got me where I am now?"

Knowing the reasons for your goals is crucial to scoring the goal. If the reason is not in line with your Production Department or if you set a goal just to make your Sales Department look good, to impress someone else, there are sure to be problems. Every step of the process will go astray. You will be saying "yes" when you mean "no" repeatedly, with a corrosive effect on your quality of life.

Some Claim That Time Is The Only Thing You Can Manage

Finally, what would a goal setting discussion be without at least a mention of time management? There are many time management systems out there, so I will not review them or put forth another one. Do some research and choose one that you like.

As a *concept* of time management, however, Stephen Covey's system, as discussed in his groundbreaking book *The Seven Habits of Highly Effective People*, is a great way to start. Covey talks about rating our activities based on their urgency and importance. He focuses special attention on the "not urgent, but important" activities. These are self-renewal activities. They include family time and other relationship building, rest, recreation, meditation and other forms of "just being," and planning and being open to recognizing new opportunities. Covey refers to these rejuvenating activities as "sharpening the saw," pointing out that a business that runs its machines without ever taking time out to service them will certainly run out of steam and fail. There are indeed urgent *and* important matters, such as crises, pressing problems and deadline-driven projects.

These urgent and important matters are the activities most people spend most of their days doing. Life, however, can become overly encumbered with these and with urgent but *un*important matters, such as interruptions, some calls, mail, meetings and reports, and many socially pressured obligations. This is why Covey recommends to *first schedule and make sacred* your renewal activities. I recommend it, too. If your time management is out of control, go back and review your whys. Usually when we are in line with our goals, we manage to prioritize well and manage our time well.

Goal-Setting With Moderation

Goal-setting always sounds like such an ambitious undertaking. It has overtones of "the beginning of greatness." It conjures up images of immense hard work and climbing ladders of success. From the details contained in this "how-tos of goal-setting" chapter, you can see that people who set goals the *CLO* way will expend some considerable energy just doing the goal-setting.

I have aimed, however, to make *CLO*-style goal-setting a tempered exercise. Correctly done, it is moderated first by *being true to yourself*. Goal-setting is not supposed to be an exercise in stretching yourself so far you become unrecognizable as yourself. Second, as I have emphasized in many ways, goal-setting should be based on building upon your *strengths*, not struggling to overcome weaknesses. Third, goal-setting should *not always* be about attaining *money, power or recognition*. Ultimately goal-setting can be in service to self-actualization, becoming your best, truest self while making a contribution to the betterment of the Earth and Humanity. Goal-setting should not be a plan to fill 18 hours a day with achievement-oriented activity, so that you become a "human doing" instead of a human being.

So make sure that "to do" lists are not so long that you cannot get them done. Be careful not to overwhelm yourself. And listen to Covey when he makes the very good point that we all burn out if we do not take the time for our own growth and to tend things like our relationships. I always think of the song, *Cat's in the Cradle* by Harry Chapin when talking about spending time with family. In the song, the father never has time for his son. Whenever the boy asks, "When you comin' home, Dad," the father replies "I don't know when, but we'll get together then, Son." When as a retiree, the father wants time with his son, the son tells his father how busy *he* now is, but that it's "sure nice" talking to him. The father then concludes, "he'd grown up just like me, my boy was just like me."

I hear many parents and partners talking about "quality time with the family," but they do not realize that there really is no substitute sometimes for just plain "quantity time." The person who is there the most is the one who gets to experience those first moments in a child's life and who gets to hear their partner's innermost thoughts and feelings. And if you have a teenager, you know that they come to you at the "strangest times" to share their life's dreams and fears. Be there! Whenever you are doing a cost-benefit analysis in your life business, make sure you take into account what each minute is really worth.

Easy Does It

All details aside, the core ideas of the hows of goal-setting are easy. Write down what the toy is, what the stairs look like, how many stairs there are, what kind of shoes you need to get up the stairs, what kind of energy you need for the climb, who else you need to support the climb, what skills you need to make the climb and what your time frame is. One step at a time toward the top of the stairs, closer and closer to the toy. The why, on the other hand, is about the belief you have in yourself and your support systems and the strength to control the impulses to "escape" and grab the first marshmallow. And get to know all of the monsters that you will meet on the way up the stairs. Most of them will be manageable with the right resources and tools, many of which you will encounter in the rest of *CLO*.

We do all need to have mindfully set goals. Be cautious about working on too many goals at one time. It is more efficient and productive to *focus* as much as you can and avoid multitasking your way through life. Finally, remember that it is okay, in fact essential, to just "be" sometimes.

Chapter 6

Why Our Ears and Tongues Do Not Always Work: Communication Part 1

We all start out knowing how to talk,
But we forget the whys and start to squawk.
There are so many reasons to communicate wrong.
If we were on a game show, we'd get the gong.

When we get past our need to be right,
It really cuts down on those pesky fights.
We must be strong enough to be weak,
So into our hearts the other can peek.

Keep in mind it's not those pretty easy hows.
The whys are what packs the punch and pows.
So look deep inside and give up the conflict.
Otherwise to resentment you will be a convict.

Take the time you need with your whys,
And all of your reasons you will categorize.
When you understand your own deep down,
You'll be ready to learn the step by step lowdown.

The Plain White Rapper

You understand Me, Inc and all of the company's departments. You have made a strategic plan and you have set goals. Before anything is implemented, Me, Inc needs to make sure that all of the departments practice good communication habits. Me, Inc cannot survive if your parts are not communicating with each other and being harmonious, or if you are not communicating with all the other Me, Incs in your life. Whenever I work with a business, many of the problems they are experiencing can be traced back to poor communication.

We Are Already Equipped

The first lesson learned when studying human behavior is that human beings "come out of the box" prepared to learn verbal communication. We are born with everything that we need to communicate with each other at the highest levels of any species on the planet. When you listen to the way people talk to each other, though, this fact seems incredible. There is shunning, ignoring, screaming and arguing to the point of wars. Sarcasm and derisive humor are the way television "rolls" now. Advertising has adopted every awful form of interaction out there to appeal to the lower instincts in our advanced species. In some interactions with the couples in my practice, I have occasionally resorted to forbidding a couple to speak to each other for a time and instead to write down everything they want to say to each other just to bypass the thoughtless, impulsive and destructive behavior that they are passing off as communication.

So, ask yourself: If listening and speaking are prepared behaviors, what is the problem with the world's communications? You will recognize the following concept from a previous chapter: It is not the How of communication, it is the Why! The good news is that when I am done discussing the whys of communication, then, in the next chapter, "Rules Of Engagement: Communication Part 2," I will show you the very simple steps to great effective communication. But first, once again forget your p's and q's for a while, just get your whys together and *listen* up.

Often when someone asks me what I do, I answer simply that "I teach people how to talk." This of course starts some very interesting conversations and always ends with my "What is wrong with the world's communication" soap box speech. So, here it is for you.

Usually when someone is not communicating well, it is because they do not want to. They choose not to for some reason. I will as always exclude those persons who have been badly neglected or abused, who truly never learned any communication skills and who were never exposed in school or elsewhere to these lessons. So assuming for the most part that we are working with individuals who have had the opportunity to learn communication skills, I will review and discuss the possible reasons for failing to engage in good communicating behavior. We need to look at this because people so often refuse to communicate well. And they often communicate poorly or not at all, even when most other people around them (and maybe they themselves) see clearly that this failure is going to have a negative impact on the poor communicator's relationships and the quality of his or her own life.

Why We Do Not Listen

The listening part of communication may not occur because the non-listener holds the simple belief that he or she is so right that there is no need to hear anyone else's opinions or facts. After all, what is the point of hearing all the information if you have already made a judgment or conclusion? Closely related is the "I want to win at any cost" type. This person is thinking, "Who cares who is right or wrong, so long as I come out on top?" A third relative of these two is the personality that says, "I am so busy that I do not have time for this babble." All three of these cousins spend most of their communication time trying to think of what they are going to say next. They just do not see any point in listening to anyone else.

Another group of people who are busy with what they are going to say next have the trademark of interrupting others or never pausing enough to allow others to speak. These people were just never listened to by others and feel desperate to be heard and understood. It is difficult for this type to have the faith that they will get a turn, so they just talk through everyone else's turns.

Another type, people who are stuck in deep-seated, maladaptive belief systems, do not listen to others because it makes them uncomfortable. Go back to the "hierarchy of needs" and tribal instincts discussed in the first Goal-Setting chapter. From your common experience, you know the expression, "self-fulfilling prophecy." The prophecies self-fulfill because we are anthropologically prepared to keep intact the belief systems of the tribe by whom we were raised. The sooner you internalize the rules and beliefs of your tribe, the sooner your belonging is secured and then the more likely you are to survive. Those members who do not support the beliefs of the tribe will be ostracized and shunned or worse. This "you don't belong" treatment is the worst form of punishment, so it feels to virtually all members of the tribe that it is in their best interest to go along with the beliefs. As humans, we are very uncomfortable with "twilight zone" feelings. Therefore, anything that contradicts the beliefs a person's tribe has instilled can be very uncomfortable and upsetting to a person who has used the beliefs to stay physically and/or psychologically safe. An example of this type of person is a woman who "just knows," probably from her family's belief system, that "all men lie." She will tend to date married men or men who perpetually break promises. She is unlikely to listen to anyone who suggests that she should look for other men. She maintains the consistency and comfort of living with the instilled "all men lie" belief by seeking and finding only such men. Similarly, people will communicate, or fail to communicate, with others in ways which validate such beliefs as, "In the end, I will be abandoned or abused," "I am not as good as others and will never be good enough" or "I will never get my emotional needs met." Even people who seem to have taken a "180" from their family of origin are probably just living out the flip side of the same coin, unless they have genuinely worked through all of the issues they had.

Why We Do Not Speak

Another anti-communication belief system is the one that states that communication just leads to conflict and to put-downs and abuse. If the tribe was always hostile to a person, then that individual usually ended up on the losing end of conflicts or took verbal or physical abuse. Convincing a person with that history to voice themselves, or listen long enough, so they can see other possibilities will be an uphill battle. This person believes speaking, or listening too long, will only give the other person time enough to "build up steam." To these people, the less said the better.

This belief is actually quite common. But as with other types, believers in "the less said the better" are protecting their belief systems, systems that include the tribal belief that what the tribe was doing was not abuse, but was instead deserved or acceptable discipline. Spanking and low levels of bullying, such as excess teasing by peers, siblings, parents or other adults, can feel like abuse to a child. This abused feeling remains, even if the tribe approves of the abusiveness and even if the child grows up to defend the actions. Many people who suffered "side effects" from trauma do not acknowledge them because their family tribe said the trauma was just acceptable behavior. They speak of the trauma with little emotion and a "no big deal" attitude.

Ironically, the people discussed will tend not to be honest and open with a mental health professional, or to not listen to that professional, for all of the same reasons we are citing for not listening to others. One of the first tasks facing a professional upon meeting a new client is enabling the client to feel it is safe to speak the unspeakable, to violate the tribal rules, to call bad or misguided treatment what it is. Remember that we do not like "twilight zone" feelings and thoughts. So if such people admit that "something was wrong," they may believe that they are admitting to being "abnormal." These feelings are compounded if there is a chance that members of their current tribe, whether it is the family-of-origin tribe or a new tribe, will ridicule them for their belief that the actions were abusive or unacceptable.

Among the effects of poor or misguided treatment early in life, there is affect intolerance, the inability to bear the discomfort of feeling one's own feelings. Affect intolerance can block both expressing oneself and listening to others. If a person is afraid of their own feelings, then they will definitely not want to communicate those feelings or listen with an empathic ear to other people's feelings.

Why We Do Not Listen Deeply

Empathy is that form of connection which is deep understanding of another person. The technique of empathy will be discussed in depth in the next chapter. It is active, responsive listening that allows the speaker to feel the listener is truly present with them. And it can be blocked in a great many ways. One of these is lack of skill; empathy is not taught in school and very few families provide good models, so many people grow to adulthood without the know-how. But here we will discuss the "why" factors that block people's drive or willingness to empathize. The same factors that block listening at all prevent empathic listening as well. If a person does not care who is right or wrong, but just wants to win, if a person simply knows he is so right he does not need to listen, if a person is "too busy" or too intent on being heard to listen, then that person will never get to the point of listening *well*.

Some people believe that empathy is too passive and/or that empathy looks like agreement. Sometimes when I demonstrate empathy to clients, and urge them to try it, they immediately shut me down with "I cannot just sit and listen and understand. I should be fixing the problem." Empathy does not fit the task-oriented framework of these people. Some people feel very uncomfortable with allowing others to talk and process and figure out on their own how to fix problems. These individuals want to grab jobs out of the hands of others and fix everything right away. Of course, this inhibits the other person's development. The "fixer" puts the "fixed" in a position of feeling dependent, "one down" and inadequate. Usually good managers and owners will see the error of this thinking. The "empathy as agreement" argument is more difficult to overcome. People who are used to conflict and to winning push back against empathy as just a "wimpy" response and a way of giving in.

"Empathy is too touchy-feely" or "We don't do touchy feely here" are common arguments from business clients and especially from people with affect intolerance. These people are used to pushing aside feelings or other "soft" things that they believe will interfere with decisions and processes. They equate empathizing and real communication with too much feeling. For these people, feelings are uncomfortable because they feel too much like unproductive time-wasting.

Identity issues often prevent empathy and communication.

Classic examples are the Hatfield-McCoy feud and the fictional Capulet and Montague families of *Romeo and Juliet*. If a person is raised in a tribe where distrusting and hating another tribe is part of the culture, then it is very difficult to overcome the belief and stop long enough to ask, "Why?" A fourth generation Hatfield may not even know why the feud existed and yet could hate. Romeo and Juliet saw death as the only way out of the dilemma created by their opposing families. If a person is raised in a culture where they believe they are very special or that others are flawed, the identity that is internalized is not conducive to listening and understanding. Add to this brainwashing the fact that we are anthropologically prepared to be suspicious of others who are different from us. It makes good sense that we would be cautious of someone who looks or acts very different from our group. This fact is why towns historically never grew too large. They stayed in the range where inhabitants could recognize everyone by sight. Malcolm Gladwell discusses our automatic, "blink" responses to strangers and to differences in his book *Blink*.

Getting At The Problem Whys In Your Particular Situation

One of the simplest methods for rooting out the whys of problematic communication is to do a cost-benefit analysis of the particular interactions that are affected by your communication problems. If you are having difficulty with your spouse, for example, take some time to step back, look at the interactions, and ask yourself each time what each of you is getting out of the process. This is Box C of the Decisional Balance Table from Chapter 5, the Pros of the Present State. Doing this investigation is based on that sometimes hard-to-swallow idea that any person doing any behavior that persists is being "paid" to do it. When communications go bad, the person or persons who are causing the problem are getting paid to do something other than good communication. So look carefully at the payoffs. In a business, we look at things like "cliques," at where the real power is in the company, and at the culture of the company. Family and friend groups have these same influences.

There are many forms of payments for people not communicating in businesses. "Snapping" and hurting people and their feelings sometimes seems safer than risking getting hurt. Payment may be higher for staying on the good side of the boss and not listening empathically to the supervisor the boss hates. Maybe it is so important to be popular and well liked by the "in" crowd that we are highly motivated to ignore the outcasts at the other lunch table. Some people can think, "I'm so cool that I will look away when the geeks walk by." At times, wit and intellect are so important that it is necessary to correct other people's grammar and to insult them when they speak incorrectly. Being right may be the only thing that matters, so it costs too much to acknowledge other people's ideas. Yelling can work so well at getting others to back down that good communication skills do not pay a big enough dividend to offset the payoff for yelling. Sometimes the fear of "causing trouble" is so scary that avoiding this pain is payment enough for the bad communication at a board room table or in an office. This list could go on and on. The important point is to look carefully at payments outside of the communication which are rewarding and reinforcing other-than-good-communication behavior. Remember that avoiding monsters and pain is the most powerful payment living creatures respond to. So do not dismiss what is "not happening" when you do the cost-benefit analysis of any communications. These "hidden agendas," what is not being spoken or admitted to, make communicating even more complicated when the number of people involved increases.

In Me, Inc and We, Inc life businesses, when you observe objectively, you will be able to ascertain the hidden agendas where there is poor communication. For example, when you and your spouse interact sarcastically or in a bashing manner, is there a group of "friends" hanging out and listening? Are they laughing at the sarcasm and derisive humor? Is there more payment in the form of peer attention and slaps on the back than the payment delivered for good relations? Or worse yet, has your spouse been paid so many times for his or her bad communication habits that he or she self-reinforces with cockiness or unhealthy belief systems? Is the fear of receiving negative comments back giving you the go ahead to speak harshly first?

For any of you who have raised more than one child, you will be able to relate to the following story that demonstrates this point. When my twin boys were about four years old, as a responsible mother, I tried to imbue them with table manners. And, yes, I defined the goal very behaviorally, so they both knew what was meant by "good table behavior." There were times, however, when the two of them would get into a "sibling state" and I would just need to concede the battle, saying to myself, "There is no payment I can come up with that is greater than brother's laughter and connection when one of them threatens to dump his vegetables into his milk." Sometimes it was even obvious, when one boy was alone, that the memory of the "payment" would urge on the fun behavior over what I considered acceptable behavior. I work with parents whose children exhibit some behaviors just to "see smoke come out of Mom's ears."

When looking to uncover a person's agenda, remember to check out the Production Department in much greater detail than the Marketing and Sales department. Sales may be saying that good communication is one of the company values, but if Production is putting out bad communication, then that person's *real* value and motives lie elsewhere. Perhaps that person's true driving force is to be right at all costs, or to put you in a one-down position. Whatever it is, there is some attempt to hide it from you, and it may even be hidden from the bad communicator's awareness. The point here is to look at the behavior that Production is putting out, not the self-serving and perhaps deliberately untrue advertising Sales is presenting.

In relationships it is important to understand other people's motives, but your own whys are more important than the other person's whys. You can do something about your own. You can only affect others' whys indirectly. When you are doing the cost-benefit analyses, make sure that you are honest with yourself. Know all the payoffs for *your own* poor communication, and know the ones for your good communication. You too probably have some "goodies" that come from bypassing some of the communication rules. This again involves Box C of the Decisional Balance Table, the Pros of the Unchanged State. Once you have discovered those, then go back and complete a whole Decisional Balance Table. You will probably be able to find some compelling payoffs to be reaped from healthy communication, or at least some negative consequences of your poor communication habits. Start with whatever motivations you have for becoming a better communicator.

You can become the best communicator you can be. And while this improvement will not guarantee that others will communicate well with you, it makes your chances better. When we get into the hows, there are some communication techniques that can boost your chances of "survival" even when you are with very poor communicators.

Hope

So the good news is that we can move forward and learn the simple Rules of Engagement for healthy communication, especially now that we understand and can start to "chip away" at our anti-communication ideas. The simplicity of good communication is why there are so many consultants out there "teaching" communication skills. They know the hows. But when a business or individual calls me in to consult about communication problems, they may not want to look at the subject matter of this chapter, the problems and pathology that block communication. The bad news they must face is that the problems and pathology exist. Otherwise their company or their family would be run and ruled by the simple skills of communication rather than being dominated by the chaos of conflict and poor communication they hire me to replace. Consultants who teach communication need to understand pathology and have a background that allows them to get beyond the "hows" to fix and repair the problematic "whys." But going back to the good news, once we get untangled from the whys, the hows are the proverbial "piece of cake."

Chapter 7

Rules Of Engagement: Communication Part 2

Now that we know why we need communication,
We'll all be able to tune to the very same station.
We all have the need to be heard and understood,
But if we all talk at once it won't be any good.

So first try to listen and understand,
Then communication will go as planned.
Go back in the box and follow the rules.
Before you know it you'll be one of the cools.

Empathy can be scored so study hard,
Be sure to let down your listening guard.
Don't give advice or pointlessly opine.
Or a very low score others will assign.

Repeat it back with your body in tow
And the speaker's face will start to glow.
Empathy's a skill that you can master,
Just don't get preachy like the local pastor.

Take the floor over with assertive speech,
For the right words and tone you should carefully reach.
Just state your point short and concise
And your life will begin to be a real slice.

The Plain White Rapper

If the departments in a business do not communicate well, products or services will never get beyond the production line or the drawing board. And the Customer Service department will mirror to the outside world the poor communication going on in their inside world. If the owners do not communicate well, the end result can be disastrous. But good communication skills are infectious. When the businesses of the world benchmark good communication, it will trickle into the We, Incs and the Me, Incs. The opposite is true also. If all of the Me, Incs and We, Incs practice and stay mindful of good communication habits, then these "businesses" will model and transfer these skills to the larger businesses.

For those who are uncertain about the value of good communication and team building, I refer to research in the medical profession. Several years ago, concerned about patient safety, the Veteran's Administration (VA) National Center for Patient Safety (NCPS) consulted the airline industry, who they believed to have the best knowledge of safety. The airline industry had found that communication and team building were very important factors in maintaining safety and preventing air disasters. They had a program called Crew Resource Management, the model of which the VA used to base their own training program, Medical Team Training. The program is founded on effective communication, teaching professionals in health care assertiveness and rules of communication that focus on respect and shared responsibility. The research on this is summarized in a review article that was published in November of 2004 in the NCPS newsletter, "TIPS."

The Core Hows

We will move into the hows of communication now, called the *Rules of Engagement.* I often laugh when people talk about "thinking outside the box" where communication is concerned. I tell them that I spend a great deal of communication training time showing people how to "go back in the box." There are very definite rules that drive good communication. They do not take creativity to understand and follow, and trying to step out of the box tends to invite breaking these basic rules.

First, there is the Golden Rule, which we all learned as children. It states simply, "Treat people the way that *you* want to be treated." This is self-explanatory and has to do with the fact that everyone wants to be respected and listened to. I hold it to be universal that people want to believe that their ideas and words are valuable and mean something in whatever tribe is home to them.

Next, there is the rule of "Listen First." If we go back to our discussion on human development, this rule sometimes seems counterintuitive. As humans, anthropologically, we need to be understood and therefore listened to. So we all have a great need to talk. But if everyone is talking at once, then nobody gets heard. If you can overcome the natural instinct to speak first, then you can become a good listener.

The definition of Accurate Empathy is "understanding the meaning, feelings, thoughts, and/or overall experience of another as if from the inside out, and conveying that understanding in a language, including nonverbal language, suitable to that other person." Good Accurate Empathy expands the speaker's self-exploration and self-understanding by adding depth, meaning or feeling to what has already been conveyed. Be clear that empathy is not agreeing, fixing, advising or sympathizing.

Imagine being able to score a person on how well they listen. Robert Carkhuff and Charles Truax, in 1969, designed a scoring system for empathic listening, called the Accurate Empathy Scale. The scale goes from a score of 1, the worst empathy and listening, to a score of 5, the best empathy and listening. Good nonverbal language is a must for good Accurate Empathy and good nonverbal behaviors enhance the score a person receives for their performance as an empathic listener. Poor nonverbals can diminish even a great verbal empathic response. Figure 7.1 is the Accurate Empathy Scale reflecting the definition of empathy above.

Figure 7.1
Accurate Empathy Scale

IF THE LISTENER		SCALE SCORE
detracts significantly from the meaning, depth or content of what has been conveyed by the speaker	the score is	1
detracts somewhat from the meaning, depth or content of what has been conveyed by the speaker	the score is	2
matches (neither adds to nor detracts from) the meaning, depth or content of what has been conveyed by the speaker	the score is	3
adds somewhat to the meaning, depth or content of what has been conveyed by the speaker	the score is	4
adds significantly to the meaning, depth or content of what has been conveyed by the speaker	the score is	5

Figure 7.2 contains examples of empathy ratings. Each situation that is described, is followed by five numbered statements that could be made in response to that situation. The numbering reflects the Accurate Empathy Scale value of the statement. Statement 1 receives a score of 1 on the Accurate Empathy Scale, very poor empathy, Statement 3 receives a score of 3, moderate, "matching level" empathy, and so forth. Take note of this Level 3, the matching or interchangeable level. It is the level that trainers urge their empathy trainees to try for when they are beginning to learn empathy. Level 3 is fairly easy to do, "nothing fancy," just a basic "response in kind" to what the speaker has said, with somewhat different wording so it avoids sounding like mimicking. And, yet, speakers feel "listened to" when receiving empathy at a level 3.

Figure 7.2
Examples Of Empathy Ratings

Situation 1: Bob has plans to go on a fishing weekend with his "school buddies." His wife, Sally, tells him that she
  thinks he and his "pals" are immature and that they should "get lives." Bob says to Sally,
  1. "Do you know where my favorite flannel shirt is?"
  2. "You are so jealous of my friends."
  3. "You seem angry that I'm going away with my friends."
  4. "You sound really angry. Are you threatened by my relationship with these guys?"
  5. "I am sensing something more than anger about this trip. Do you feel like I don't pay enough attention to you,
     or does this remind you of the way your father treated your mother?"

Situation 2: Irene is a supervisor. She calls to Denise in front of four other employees and harshly reprimands her for
  forgetting one page of the report she placed on Irene's desk. Denise says to Irene,
  1. "I can't believe that you would yell at me in front of everyone!"
  2. "I thought I put the whole report there, let me check."
  3. "It sounds like you are really angry over the mistake."
  4. "You seem very angry over this mistake. Is there something else you are angry at me about, too?"
  5. "You are very angry about this mistake. Could it be that you are feeling a lot of pressure about this whole
     project?"

Situation 3: An employee says to his supervisor, "I'm not clear on the overall mission or goal behind this project.
  I'm not hesitant about my abilities. I know I can perform. I'm just blocked and do not have much done
  because I'm not sure where the CEO wants to end up." The supervisor says to the employee,
  1. "We really just need to get to work!"
  2. "You're upset, but just suck it up."
  3. "It sounds like you are really confused."
  4. "You seem really confused because you know you can perform well, but the direction is ambiguous."
  5. "I can see that you are confused and blocked, but it's not about your abilities. I sense that you are anxious
     about approaching the CEO to clarify."

Situation 4: Don says to Tom, "I don't want her to find out that the group didn't like her ideas. It will just hurt her
  feelings." Tom says to Don,
  1. "Who cares?"
  2. "You're such a softy."
  3. "It sounds like you are worried about her."
  4. "I'm sensing that you have a need to protect her from the truth."
  5. "You seem to need to protect her from the truth. And it looks like it's hard for you to see
     how this could ever be worked through to a good ending."

Situation 5: Dana says to Jane, "He undermined my authority again and just took the project out of my hands!
  But there is *no point* in *saying* anything. He'll just get angry." Jane says to Dana,
  1. "You need to go out with us after work."
  2. "He always does the same thing."
  3. "Sounds like you feel helpless."
  4. "I can hear that you are disappointed and frustrated and that you feel powerless to do anything."
  5. "I can see that you're frustrated by this pattern. I'm sensing though that your helplessness is coming from a
     belief that something catastrophic will happen if you are assertive with him."

As you can see, the responses that distracted attention away from what the speaker was saying, or gave unsolicited advice, produced the lowest scores. The level 3 empathic responses were for the most part just feeding back what the speaker was saying, but in slightly different words. This level lets the speaker know that the listener heard what was said. If the listener remains attentive and ready, the speaker is likely to feel safe and welcome to tell more. Listeners can improve their scaled score by "peppering" in some great body language, as discussed next. If you never progress beyond Level 3 verbal responses but boost their value with good nonverbal behavior, you should meet most speakers' needs to be listened to.

The Nonverbal Contribution

First, eye contact is essential to good empathy. It should be soft and welcoming, not piercing or constant. The listener's eyes need to be on the same "level" or height as the speaker's eyes. Otherwise the anthropological message becomes one of power. Even though we can think beyond our old messages, tall people are considered dominant. In fact, as pointed out in Malcolm Gladwell's book, *Blink*, they even make more money than short people. Sit down so that the speaker and listener are at the same level.

The second component involves arm and hand gestures. These need to be open and inviting. No finger pointing or arm folding. The final component of good empathic nonverbal behavior is the position of the listener's body in relation to the speaker. It should be almost straight on, face to face, not side by side or angled away. Next time you are in a restaurant, notice that pairs who are talking usually sit opposite each other. It is the best position for good communication.

People who are trying to impress will quote research that states body language accounts for over 50 percent of what is conveyed. Stop and reframe this. When you do not know a person well, the body language is very important because you do not have much to go on. People who know each other very well tend to let some "less than perfect" body habits slip, because they are focusing on the content of the communication. But when you really want someone to feel understood, make sure that you "checklist" your body language.

Most important, though, is to have a Production Department that is genuinely interested in what the other person has to say. Then your Sales Department will be able to advertise the excellent product of good listening skills that are coming more easily and naturally because you truly care to understand.

The Impact Of Empathy

When selling something to a business, a good sales person goes in and listens at least 70 percent of the time. Obviously, the "prospect," or person who invited the sales person in, is having some issue and that is why the sales person is there. This is how the prospect's problems are uncovered and brought to light. The most important thing for the sales person to find out is whether his or her product is the solution to the problem the prospect is having. In other words, the sales person's hope is that the product fulfills a need that the prospect has. Unless the sales person listens empathically and asks clarifying questions, he or she will never "drill down" to the solution.

When *your* Sales Department is listening to a speaker, keep in mind that your job is primarily to drill down to what this person is really saying. On the surface, the prospect or speaker may say, "I am not sleeping well at night." Now if all you care about is showing that your Production Department can solve sleeping problems, you may respond with, "Why don't you just borrow some of your mother's sleeping pills?" If the person gives you a blank stare or makes an excuse to walk away, it is because you tried to solve a problem before the real problem was revealed. If your physician did this, you might accuse him or her of malpractice. If as the listener, you said, "Sounds like sleeping is a problem and I know how difficult the day can be when you don't get enough sleep," the speaker would hear you really saying, "I heard what you said and you can go ahead and tell me more." Notice there was no opinion, just listening, understanding and proving that this process was going on. In the end, after some more interactions, the listener may find out that a new factory moved in next door and is making noise all night. Sleeping pills are not the answer. Or it may be revealed that there is some anxiety over a potential job loss or illness. The only way to find out what a person is **really** saying is to listen, understand and prove it by summarizing. In the summarizing, if you know the person well, you can go deeper. This can be seen from the statements that received scores of 4 and 5 in the Figure 7.2 examples. For the sleeping problem, a good friend or spouse may be able to say, "It sounds like you are tired. I know that you get panicky when you start to lose sleep."

It is understandable that we have the urge to talk or to think about what we are going to say next. Many of us also want to jump in to "fix" the problem right away. Much of the time, though, with the right listener, people can come up with their own solutions. This is more empowering and self-esteem building than having the solution provided. If I am selling my product to a prospect, he or she is much more likely to buy the product and to use the product according to specifications if the meeting ends with the prospect saying, "You know, that machine you sell is exactly what I need to solve my production line slowdowns." In families, the children and other "direct reports" are much more likely to buy into your programs if you use empathy and questioning to direct them to solutions. A question to a teenager of "How is that decision going to impact your life?" is far more powerful than a lecture on the negative effects of their desires. This will be especially true if the relationship has been based on mutual listening and the parent is permitted to follow up with, "Can I tell you what I would do?" Teach your direct reports, including your spouse, to do cost-benefit analyses and you are more likely to "make the sale." This teaching is done with empathic listening, followed by respectful, well-grounded talk.

Further Details Of Empathic Listening

As you probably noticed, the only "I" statements allowed in empathy are ones that involve reflection, such as "I hear you saying," "I believe you are trying to say," and "I didn't really understand what you were trying to say, so can you try re-phrasing it?" Avoid giving an opinion during the time you are the listener. In the *Empathy and Communication Training* manual and DVD that we have our partner clients use, we include a piece of floor tile, so that the speaker and listener are reminded of who "has the floor." The speaker can gently remind the listener "I have the floor" if the listener tries to give an opinion, lend some advice or compete for attention and the speaker role.

There are some final "warnings" for empathic listening. Your tone and body language must match your words. If what you are saying is sad, then you must not be smiling. Ask questions if you do not understand, *at the point when you do not understand*. It will set back and add frustration to the communication process if you wait until seven statements in to say that you did not understand something back at the second statement. Only give advice when it is asked for, or after much listening and then "asking permission", as in inquiring gently, "Can I give you some suggestions?" If you are off-base with your empathy or advice, just back up and try again. Do not get defensive when the person corrects, or even becomes a bit irritated with your misunderstanding.

Empathy is a powerful tool for those who want to become communication craftspeople, but it also serves another important job, that of "keeping the heat out" of interactions. Even if it initially invites more anger in the speaker when the listener says, "It seems like you are very angry with me," eventually the speaker will probably stop and talk about what is going on under the anger, *if you stay with the empathy and do not start firing anger back*. Empathy works a little like the martial arts tactic of stepping aside and letting your attacker fall over from his own momentum, or smash his fist into the wall instead of into your face. The person who is aggressing only receives self-inflicted pain and the other person avoids injury. Empathy will also keep *you* from becoming irrational. If you are focused on empathizing and communicating well, it is less likely that you will be overcome with emotions, especially anger. The old adage, "It takes two to tango" really is true.

Assertiveness: What It Is and Why The World Needs It

You have observed the first Rule of Engagement, the Golden Rule, and the second, to Listen First. When you are done listening and it is your turn to "have the floor," your job is to use the third Rule of Engagement, Assertive Communication. Don't worry. There are strict guidelines and rules for this technique, too. Stay in the box for a while. Assertiveness can range anywhere from quick, business-like statements all the way to formally planned and rehearsed statements, depending on the seriousness of the issue and nature of the relationship.

The definition of assertiveness is "Communication that expresses your thoughts and feelings clearly and straightforwardly, takes into account your rights and needs, and respects the rights and needs of the other person or people." It falls on a continuum, between unassertiveness and aggression, as can be seen in Figure 7.3.

Figure 7.3
Assertiveness Continuum

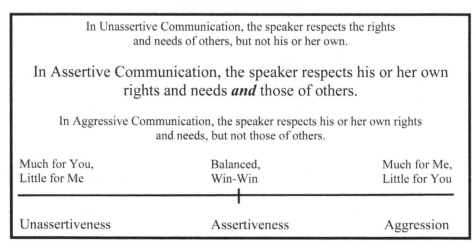

While assertiveness is a way of encouraging honesty and accountability, it is a relative term, depending on the situation. When an acquaintance asks if you like her new dress, it is certainly acceptable to just say, "Yes." If a person that you are involved with asks a similar question, it is much better for the relationship in the long term if you are honest. This issue of course brings up much controversy when coaching or speaking. It is amazing how often when dealing with multiple business owners or couples, I hear an unassertive response like, "I don't want to hurt any feelings," as an excuse for not telling the truth, even when it is about an important issue. In a case like this, the truthful statement would really look more like, "I don't want to get involved," or "I don't want to be disliked or disapproved of," or "I don't want to suffer the repercussions of (*whatever the called-for statement or action is*)." And on and on. Remember, it is not the how, it is the why!

More people die every year from unassertiveness than from aggression. Look at the numbers. In 1964, one man stabbed Kitty Genovese in New York City, in a murder that took an estimated 15 minutes to complete, while 38 people watched and did nothing. How many bystanders watched the two teens travel with the toddler in 1993 in England, abusing him all the way in plain view of dozens of people for over an hour, before they killed him? Hit and run accidents are all about unassertiveness. Obviously the driver does not want to be honest and accountable. When teens abandon the person at the party who later dies from alcohol poisoning or a drug overdose, it is about the unassertiveness of not owning up to their involvement. Instead of dialing 911 and admitting to the "bad behavior," they run. So many professionals ignored child abuse that it became necessary to create a law that mandates the reporting of suspected abuse.

Next time you are unassertive, ask yourself "If I get into trouble, do I really want to have helped create a world where doing nothing is the norm?" Think about the number of times we hear, "I can't say that because I don't want to hurt any feelings." What happens when it is the supervisor in a manufacturing company that makes medical equipment saying it about an employee who has not reached the level of performance and sanitary procedures expected after six months of employment?

By the point where we see a bully at his worst, it is likely that we are seeing the results of years of the people around him "doing nothing" and "not getting involved." By then he has been paid for this behavior multiple times. Does anybody really think that Hitler or Saddam Hussein started out with the amount of power that they had when they tried to destroy the world? No, of course not! They were given that power systematically over the years. I am not suggesting that people stand up alone to dangerous, explosive criminals or bullies. What I am suggesting is that we stand up to them *before* they become dangerous. Stop paying them to behave badly. It is obvious to see what the payoff for aggressive communication was and is. The bully gets paid for the aggression by everyone else "shutting up" and giving in. Eventually, the bully learns that the quicker he or she escalates the loudness and aggression, the quicker his or her desires and "entitlements" are honored and granted.

Expect Resistance and Rewards

On the flip side, the payoffs for unassertiveness are either "becoming invisible," quickly escaping the situation, placating and/ or befriending the bully or being seen as "nice." There are almost always at least short-term costs to saying "no" to a bully or other over-controlling person. Usually, though, in the long run, the results are good. Look at the relationship as a system. Systems usually fight change. When the group or spouse or anybody starts to stand up to an aggressive person or group, the whole system will fight back. Change is scary and difficult, and besides, what bully or controller is likely to voluntarily give up the kind of power he or she has enjoyed? Whenever I work with a woman who is in a difficult or challenging relationship, I always warn her about the possible outcomes of our work. One, she may become assertive and strong and the other person or people will begin to respect her rights and make some changes, too. That is the hoped for result. Two, she may become assertive enough to leave the system that does not respect her. Three, she may become assertive enough that she can continue fighting and the system will just quiet down or the bully may leave because he or she cannot stand the new system. Finally, the system may fight back so much that she will run "screaming" from me and our work. Interestingly, when warned of the possibilities, clients are more likely to talk through the tough times and stick it out.

Bullies and controllers will usually escalate their loudness, aggression and control when the changes are new. When that does not work, they will typically try breaking down and crying. If the system is strong enough to say "No" to these escalations, and the bully or controller stays, then the whole system benefits. Even the bullies may end up thanking the change artist later. One of the good side effects of teaching assertiveness to the people around a bully is that the bully's relationships get better too. After all, it may be easier and more comfortable for the bully to "rule the world," but it is not conducive to deep loving relationships and it is ultimately not safe. The long term effects of bullying include creating angry people who in the end just want to "bring down" the bully.

The Hows Of Assertiveness

Now we can move on to the hows of assertive communication. Understand that the whys will keep popping up whenever the system fights back. Catch yourself when you start thinking any anti-assertive thoughts, like, "Oh well, he's just in a bad mood," or "I'll let the disrespect go this time." It is time to consider assertiveness training when people find themselves thinking thoughts like, "I am not strong enough," "Nobody will listen to me anyway," "I can't say anything because I don't know exactly what all of the possible outcomes are," "I don't have the right to speak up," "He's more important than I am," "Boys will be boys," "They were just having fun and kidding around," or "I don't have the skills to articulate my ideas." As with any other issue, the first step to assertiveness is to complete a Decisional Balance Table. You will then be mindful of the whys and can make sure that your reasons for becoming assertive are more powerful than your reasons for staying unassertive or aggressive. A warning here is that if a person is dangerous, get away! Do a cost-benefit analysis. If assertiveness will put you in physical danger, escape! Then if you do act, take action from a safe distance, with authorities to help you if needed.

Unlike empathy, assertive communication does involve many "I" statements. We will start with the formal planned type of assertiveness. In this type of assertive communication, you plan a time when you and the other person will have privacy for the interaction. If you are an "assertiveness novice," write down the issue in terms of an "I" statement. For example, "I don't like it that you drive so fast." Now, write down the feelings you have about the issue and *why* you have the feelings, such as "I get scared when you drive so fast *because* I think we will have an accident." Next, write down your request, being as behavioral as possible, such as "I need you to change the way you drive and slow down to within 5 miles per hour of the speed limit." Finally, write down the consequences, either negative or positive, such as "If you do not slow down, I will not ride with you anymore," and/or "If you grant this request, I will be more likely to go places with you."

A good assertive statement helps the other person do a cost-benefit analysis of their own behavior. Research done by Ellen Langer in 1978 demonstrated that when the word "because" is used in a request, people tend to comply with the request more than when the word is not used. Pollsters always let you know they are asking you questions *because* "I'm conducting a survey." "Honey, I'd like you to come to the retirement party because I will not know anyone there" works the same way.

The Five-Step Assertiveness Formula consists of:

1. A clear behavioral description of the act or pattern that you want to have changed. If you are stating something that you do not like, keep your "not likes" behavioral and do not make them about the person's character or personality. In other words, "You are a pervert" is unacceptable, while "I do not like it that you stare at me and look me up and down" is an assertive statement.

2. The feelings this behavior leads you to experience, but stated in a way that is not accusing. Avoid "you make me feel" or "your behavior makes me feel." Instead, just connect the behavior and your feelings with a "when" or time- or event-related statement like "I feel embarrassed when you make jokes about me to your friends" or "I still feel very upset that you have not changed behavior X yet." "Yet," by the way, is an encouraging little word. If used with an upbeat tone, it implies that you are anticipating a change, looking forward to it, allowing the possibility that it will occur.

3. Your "because" statement, the reasons you feel that feeling when the particular behavior occurs.

These first three parts can be used by themselves if you are not yet ready to request what you want to happen. If you are ready to "place your order," however, you go on to state:

4. What you want to see happen and perhaps a statement of good things that are likely to occur if you get what you want.

5. What you are willing to do or what will naturally happen if you do not get what you want.

Figure 7.4 contains some examples of assertive speaking.

Figure 7.4
Assertive Communication Examples

Example 1

I don't like it that you talk negatively about me to your friends.

It makes me feel unappreciated because it gives the impression you think
    that I am inferior.

I want you to start talking positively about me.

When you talk more positively about me and our relationship,
    I will be happier and want to make you happier.

If you do not change the way you talk, I will stop going places with you.

Example 2

It bothers me that you do not speak up and tell me what you need more often.

I feel alone and responsible for everything when you do not assert yourself.

I think I feel this way because I see you as sitting on the sidelines
    of our relationship.

I want you to overcome your fear of speaking up and I will work to help you
    feel safer to talk.

If you do, I will want to spend more time with you.

If you will not work on this, though, I will need to find other people to talk to
    and it will interfere with our time together.

Example 3

I get very afraid when you raise your voice, even if it is not at me, because it
    feels like the angry home I grew up in. It also scares me because I am not
    sure I can be around you if you do not at least cut down on getting loud.

I need to see that you are really working on this. I will be glad to help you if I
    can, but I want to see that you care enough about my feelings to try to fix
    this even if you think I am being too sensitive.

If you will show me you will try, I will be able to share more of my feelings
    with you like you have said you want me to. But I need to be willing to
    keep them to myself if you keep insisting that loud is just the way you talk.

No False Threats Or Promises

It is important to follow through with the last parts of the
Assertive Communication Formula. These are the "bottom line"
statements, what good will come if you get what you want, and
what you will do if you do not get what you want. If you constantly
make false threats or false promises, people will begin to know you
as insincere and will not trust your word. Your reputation as a false

promise- or false threat-maker will decrease what power you do have in the relationship. In other words, bluffing may work in a card game, but not in communication within serious relationships, whether business or intimate. Unfortunately, we do not always have the power to deliver a consequence, but if you do not have this power, do not bother to make threats. It will just block your mental and spiritual access to the upcoming possibilities.

Just because something looks hopeless at the time does not mean that it will remain that way. Situations sometimes change and you may be able to think of a way out of the circumstance. Hearing yourself use healthy assertive statements can be empowering, too. And amazingly, sometimes the person you are speaking to just needs to hear that you would like something to change. The path of least resistance is usually to just keep doing the same thing. So if the other party has been getting paid to be aggressive or to ignore other people's feelings, then that person may have just been maintaining a status quo that was working for him. When you change *You* and your part of the status quo, the person on the other end may suddenly discover a motive to change. Another positive side effect of the courage to speak up is that often others wanted to speak up assertively too, but were avoiding being the first to go.

The formal assertiveness formula is sometimes inconvenient to use. At those times, or when *spontaneous* assertiveness is necessary, remember to empathize first, then speak honestly in a tactful, gentle way. A business example of a quick efficient statement might be, "I understand that you are tired of working long hours. Right now, I must ask that you put in the extra hours until this current order goes out." A We, Inc example might be, "I know that you really get lonely when I have to be out at School Board meetings so many nights a week. This is just a really busy time with elections coming up. Can you just bear with me about two more weeks, when we can get back to a normal schedule?"

Whenever possible, businesses get "buy in" from the employees for good communication and for company policies. When I work with a company, the leaders have a retreat to write a "Code of Conduct" that applies to everyone from owners on down. Employees are much more likely to honor HR policies if they believe that the owners and upper managers have codes and rules that apply to all, including the owners and managers. This point is of major importance to We, Inc. The direct reports of We, Inc are only likely to respect the type of communication that is modeled to them. Leaders must be willing to walk the walk as well as talk the talk. The first rule in the "new code" that we work on is that there can be no triangulation. Recall from Chapter 4 that triangulation is when a person talks about another person without that person present. Under the new code, the absent party in the triangle is brought in as soon as possible. The incident is reported to the supervisor or to the other owners, not in a tattletale kind of way but with the aim of bringing all relevant parties together for discussion. Codes of Conduct also prohibit sarcasm and above all else, there is no condescension or disgust allowed. We are preprogrammed to feel shame when people express disgust toward us. Disgust carries with it the threat of shunning and casting out from the tribe. The threat of being cast out is felt as life-threatening in our deep, caveperson recesses. And it is inexcusable for people to use it in business with any of their direct reports or in a group where others may laugh and ridicule in gang-like ways.

Remember that your children are your direct reports and in many ways, your spouse is one of your direct reports. When the "bosses" think that sarcasm and poor communication tactics are funny, such as we see portrayed on so many television shows now, then it is quite unrealistic to expect the direct reports to honor communication codes. In some circles, the most usual method of getting a laugh is to use sarcasm and "one-downing." Responses like "duh" to indicate that a person is being obtuse or obvious is considered very funny. Unfortunately, the person on the bad end of this expression is feeling shame and may eventually feel anger and want revenge.

Be Clear

A vitally important point about your speaking part is to be clear and unambiguous. We are anthropologically prepared to interpret ambiguity negatively. Think about it. When our ancestors heard a suspicious noise, the ones who ran for the trees just because it made gut-level sense were the ones who survived to breed and become our ancestors. The ones who said, "Well, it may just be some enjoyable nature sound" had a greater chance of being eaten and a smaller chance of passing on their genes. Have you ever heard of a husband whose wife made the ambiguous statement, "Honey, we need to talk," say that he thought that she was being romantic? When you hear the ambiguous message, "The boss wants to see you," your first thought is probably not, "Oh, great, I'm about to get my raise!"

Interaction Styles

With the fourth Rule of Engagement we revisit precious metals. It is The Platinum Rule of "Treat people the way they want to be treated." The Platinum Rule is based on the fact that we all have a different "style" of interaction. People *feel most comfortable* interacting using a particular style, and having others interact with them using styles that are complementary to their own style. They may be able to adopt other styles, but they have their favorite, most comfortable one. Some people like to chit chat and mix socializing, storytelling and expression of feelings with work. Some people just like to "get down to business." Some people like to get results while others like to attend to details. Some people want the team to be close and always working together, while some people do not "play well with others" and like to stir up debates and conflicts. Some people want control, others want to follow. Some people fear change, while others fear disapproval. Some people draw their energy from being around people, while others get "peopled out" and need solitude. I use the DiSC assessment instrument through Inscape Publishing for evaluating styles. The letters stand for the styles of Dominance, Influence, Steadiness and Conscientiousness. The theory behind this instrument involves two belief systems that people have in varying degrees. One is about how friendly or unfriendly we believe the environment is. The other is about how much power we believe we have over our environment, or whether we believe that we have an effect upon our surroundings, especially the people in those surroundings.

Once everyone understands their own interaction style and the interaction styles of the people that they work and live with, good communication becomes a more likely possibility. Understanding your beliefs and interaction comfort levels, and the beliefs and interaction comfort levels of those around you, helps you to determine natural tendencies toward assertiveness and other interaction behaviors. Communication for Me, Inc is the same as in a business. Your own departments must communicate, but you must communicate with the other people in your life as well. The people you live with are just like the other owners in a multiple owner business. You are all in some way glued together and you must find a way to manage the property that you share and the people who are there. When consulting with a business it always helps to have all of the owners and employees take the DiSC assessment to determine their interaction style. This is combined with assessing for conflict styles within the business. Many people believe that conflict is bad, when in fact conflict is necessary to all change and progress. Like dynamite, another substance that was invented for the good, conflict can be used to destroy and it can be managed in an unsafe and destructive way. If, however, it is managed well, conflict can produce miracles. In a business, no new products would ever be designed if there were no conflict. Ideas would die inside of the person who had them if they could not risk conflict by "putting them out there." Ask yourself what your conflict style is. When you approach a situation where there is any potential conflict, do you tend to give in to the other person, just avoid any mention of the issues, fight to be right, think win-win, or try to find a solution that gets everyone part of what they want? This will tell you something about your conflict style.

The Box To Stay In

If you are not "naturally" good at communication, it may take a lot of practice, and the overcoming of fears and excuses, to begin executing skilled empathy and assertiveness. As you struggle with getting the words out, and pairing the appropriate nonverbal behavior with the words, you will need to be willing to restate yourself, so you can refine your message and be understood. The work is worth it, however, both because it will get easier with practice and because the elements of good communication are simple, really. They are:

strive first to *understand and express that understanding with active, empathic listening*; uphold your own rights and needs, and respect those of others, as you *speak assertively*; and work to *be clear and unambiguous*.

As always, the hows of communication are easy, perhaps not immediately easy to do, but certainly easy to see and grasp. Till the fields before you try to plant seeds by being clear on your whys. When having trouble communicating, ask yourself:

- "Why am I not communicating well *in this situation?*" (You may have difficulty communicating almost everywhere, or the difficulty may not be so huge and only appear in certain, limited situations.)
- "If I am hesitant to change this, why?"
- "If I think I am ready to change this, but the change is still not happening, why?"
- "What is the payment I am receiving for poor communication?"
- "What rewards and payments am I failing to see in positive communication?"

Be very clear on the causes of poor communication. If you are having chronic communication problems with someone in your life, it is unlikely that the cause is simple lack of skill. It is more likely "lack of will," that is, the other person and/or you have some pathology in the way. It may be a slight one, but it is there. Stop looking for other causes and solve the problems.

Even in the most severe conflict, communication can be healthy. There can be agreements to disagree. Compromises can be struck, where all parties get part of what they want. Or you can agree to do the work involved in finding Win-Win deals, where solutions are sought which are better for everyone than what anyone brought to the table originally. Or there can be termination of the alliance. I have worked with couples, some of whom eventually split, but who discovered along the way that they felt and got along the best when they were *talking openly about how awful their relationship was!* And some of the couples who learned to talk openly about the poor State of their Union stayed together *because they learned to talk openly.*

A hardcore, so-difficult-to-swallow truth is that people communicate poorly *because they want to.* In other words, they want something else more than they want to communicate well and resolve conflict. For example, as discussed previously, when a business bully is ruling the boardroom and everyone is cowering to his wishes, we would not expect him to "change his evil ways" too readily. He is shutting everyone else down and getting his own way the easy way. But when we look a little bit deeper, we realize that the other owners, the other "kids on the playground", are getting something out of the interactions, too. Whenever you hire someone to consult with you about poor communication, be sure that they can drill down to *why the individual poor communicators and the whole system* are malfunctioning. This applies to two-person couple systems, to huge business organizations, and to every system in between.

Ideal communication is the result of a simple-to-grasp and easier-the-more-you-practice-it four-step process:

- Follow the Golden Rule.
- Listen with empathy.
- Speak honestly, clearly and assertively.
- Follow the Platinum Rule

Chapter 8

Create Unsinkable Relation-*Ships*: Value Propositions Of Relationships

We both started out as a Me, Inc.
Now we want to become a We, Inc.
We both get our lists and start to shop,
'Cause it's time to do an in-depth value prop.

I never looked at love like this before
But this time around I want so much more.
I've seen your Sales Department here and there.
Now with me all your departments you will share.

So get all your benefits and features in a row,
It's time for some really honest tell and show.
Make sure that you get in a good disposition,
'Cause we have to hunker down and do a Value Proposition.

The Plain White Rapper

We know that a business must have a Sales Department with promotional material that matches the other departments, and that the business must tweak and improve its products, but only in the direction of its own vision. It must aim to *satisfy* the needs of customers but never *become* what "someone else wants." We know that businesses must listen to their employees and customers and that they must communicate effectively. We know that a business must set goals according to "who and what we really are," and that a business must make plans to meet its goals. Once the business has accomplished all of these things, it is time for the selling process, the matching of its products to those prospects it sells to. This is about relationships.

Relationships and Business

From the ground up, businesses eat, sleep and breathe relationships. Hiring employees, retaining employees, managing and supervising employees, selling to the customers, buying from vendors, paying taxes, renting or buying the place of business, and everything else imaginable hinges on the relationships. So once a business has defined itself and its strengths, understands its own culture and "style," has all of its departments in sync with each other, has set its goals and made a strategic plan to take steps toward these goals, has a Sales Department that honestly sings the praises of the products, and has mastered the communication skills of the organization, what is next?

There is a very good sales training program, Sandler Sales Training, which answers this question for businesses. They have processes that include "Upfront Contracts" and "Qualifying or Disqualifying the Prospect." While it may seem like just plain common sense that not every prospect is a good one for a salesperson to pursue, it is very difficult for sales people to walk away from a potential sale. And yet this excellent program teaches sales people to walk away if there is not a good fit between the prospective buyer's needs and the seller's product or service. In other words, in Sandler Sales Training, a sales person would learn to listen for the prospect's problems and issues, or "pain," and to continue the process only if the sales person's product can "solve" the problem, or relieve the pain. Sandler has an expression that brings this idea home: "No pain, no sale." If the customer has a pain and the sales person's product can relieve it, then the process continues to the next qualifying step, that of Budget. Does the prospect have the money for the product? If yes, then are there other expenditures that need to be checked into? For example, certain products, like new computer systems or software, or other new pieces of equipment, require a great deal of training to use. Some products, like diversity training, require a culture change. Some products, like new trucks, require "collateral" expenses for garaging the trucks, getting them serviced, and so forth. If all of these issues are addressed to satisfaction, then there is a good chance that the product and the prospect are a great fit and that the seller and the buyer will have a very long and fruitful relationship.

Before any of the qualification begins, however, the sales person needs to be sure that he or she is talking to and negotiating with the "Decision Maker." In other words, when selling, a sales person does not want to be talking to someone in the company who cannot actually buy the product. There are many people in a business who could benefit from a product and who can go out and shop around among many producers. But sometimes these people only have the decision-making power to eliminate producers from the list. In other words, they can say "no," but they do not have the power to say "yes" and actually spend the company money. Or these people can only go back and report their findings to someone higher up in the organization. Sandler Sales trains sales people to go directly to the decision maker in the business. And finally, before any negotiations begin, Sandler Sales people have "Upfront Contracts." This means that they are open about who they are and what they are doing. Nobody's time is wasted with this system. Both the sales person and the prospect know at each juncture of the negotiations what is happening and what they are each responsible for doing before the next step.

So a good sales person starts every relationship by informing the prospect of the steps. The first step is to proclaim honestly that he or she is interested in selling. In fact, some sales people start the initial telephone call with, "This is a sales call. You can hang up now, but if you have an open mind, I would like to take just a couple of minutes for you to hear what I have to say." Bold, but it is really "upfront" and there is no chance for a misunderstanding. The next step is to have an agenda and a list of responsibilities for each person. For example, a sales person might say the following to a prospect: "I would like about 30 minutes of your time. In this meeting, I would like to ask some questions and find out some of your needs. I'm sure that you will want to know what my products can do for you and your company. Is there anything else that you will need?"The sales person will ask the prospect very directly if he or she is a decision maker and if not, will suggest that they include the decision maker in the meeting. Finally, the sales person will discuss how comfortable the prospect feels about saying "no" if there is not a good fit. Good sales people want to make sure that they are not "strung along" because a prospect has assertiveness issues. At each juncture, the sales person discusses an agenda for the next meeting and ends the meeting by stating what is expected of him or her and what is expected of the prospect. A meeting may end with the sales person saying, "I will contact the supplier of that storage system you need and I will need you to get the exact measurements of the warehouse. Let's set our next meeting for a week from Thursday if that works for you."

Not only is the Sandler System smart, but also ethical. This system avoids sales people who can only see the money and their own benefits, the type that might continue in desperation trying to sell a product to a prospect who should have been disqualified for a budgetary reason, for lack of pain, or because the sales person's product is not the solution to relieve the pain that is there. Sandler knows that this type of behavior causes frustration, wasted time, hurt feelings and sometimes serious conflict. It leads to distrust which makes it extremely unlikely the sales person or his or her company will ever be invited to sell to that prospect again.

In most cases, a sales person sells to a prospect and they each keep their respective roles. Occasionally, though, they switch roles. Sometimes a sales person wants to buy from a prospect. They then take turns selling to each other. This makes for a somewhat more complicated relationship. But in the end, even if it is not a perfect fit both ways, the relationship does not necessarily have to hurt if only one sale is made. A slightly more complicated business selling relationship happens when two sales people want to collaborate on a sale. For example, if one person sells garages and the other person sells trucks to put in the garages, they may decide that forming a strategic alliance and selling as a team would work for them. Here again, even if the collaboration does not work, the two can either just go back to the relationship as it was or walk away. But probably the most complicated business relationship occurs when two or more people decide to co-own a business. If you have any experience with family-owned or multiple-owner businesses, then you know that while these situations can sometimes be wonderful, they can also become nightmares.

I give this background only to demonstrate that the business of selling, partnering, forming temporary working relationships (the strategic alliances referred to above) and "dancing together" in the different combinations of relationships that can exist are not simple processes. It requires the honesty of upfront contracts. It means keeping the interests of all parties in mind. And it requires a willingness to walk away from a sale or business arrangement when it does not fit. The underpinning of all this is the Value Proposition, which can be defined as a clear understanding of what each party is getting out of the sale or arrangement. And what I am about to suggest is that Value Propositions are an excellent way to help make good judgments and "honest bargains" in personal as well as business relationships.

Value Propositions and Relationships

There is probably more written about relationships than about any other subject in the world. And no wonder, since they are also one of the most complicated subjects. Every other topic discussed in this book will play into this chapter. But I am not going to talk about how you may be from different planets than your spouse or how we all have different interaction styles or how we are having trouble with understanding other generations. Those may all be true. But there is something that is indisputably true: *We only stay actively involved in relationships that we are getting something out of.* As with motivation generally and with communication, we will talk about the hows and the whys of relationships. But mostly we are going to discuss Value Propositions.

Good sales training is always based on Value Propositions. In other words, in selling and buying we need not only to look at the money to be laid out to acquire a product, we need also to do a serious cost-benefit analysis and figure out what the product is worth to the whole system and in the long run. The cost of a product is how much money you put out in the immediate. The value of a product takes into consideration the performance of the product over time. In other words, looking at only the cost is like looking at a new roof as costly because it is just a "bunch of expensive beams and shingles." A Value Proposition takes into account the fact that the roof will protect the house and all of its contents for the next 30 years or more.

Take the example of a couple that wants to enter into relationship coaching with me. Let us assume that over the period of the several months of coaching it will take to help them, the cost will come to about the same as a week-long vacation in the sun. I encourage them to do Value Propositions on the vacation and the coaching. The vacation provides a much needed break, they get along well on vacations, the kids will love it, and they all get great memories. In all likelihood, however, they will come back and start fighting again, as they have upon returning to familiar surroundings and routines after other vacations. The coaching is hard work, it takes time for the appointments and time for the homework the couple is assigned, and it may be emotionally painful. But with the work and the commitment, the couple probably will begin to communicate like never before, start dating again, and become friends again. When these things happen, the kids will be relieved, will behave better at home, and will show enhanced school performance. Do the math! If everyone would go through this process for all of their purchases, people would be much more sensible with their buying habits. But better yet, what I am going to propose now is that we use this process whenever we are going to enter into relationships and to evaluate our existing relationships. Imagine life if you did a Value Proposition on each of the relationships in your life.

When I consult with a business, I use the Value Proposition process to coach the people involved in choosing partners to be co-owners or co-managers. Many times, the potential partner has come up through the ranks. The problem is that the skills that make a good employee usually do not transfer to managing or to ownership. For example, an employee in the IT department of a company who is very good at his job, but who has no people skills, should not be promoted to management. If an established company policy dictates that after a specified length of time as an employee, a management position is automatically offered, then that policy needs to be changed. The mistake of the existing business owners inviting in new co-owners of the wrong kind can be costly and difficult, and may cause injury or can even be fatal to the business. Many owners assume that just because an employee is hard working, highly competent, and produces many "billable hours," that person is ownership material.

The company decision makers need to stop and realize that only "Rainmakers" should be put on an owner track. A Rainmaker is a person who brings new dollars into the business. I have watched many times while someone argued that an employee should be promoted to owner status because he or she "makes so much money for the company" when in fact the employee's revenue stream was all part of the daily operations. In other words, they did a job for which the company received money, and probably a lot of money if the employee is now being considered for ownership status. But the employee did not bring in new customers or increase sales in any way, and the outcome would have been the same no matter what competent person had been in that employee's position. Such a person makes an excellent employee and is an asset to the company. He or she should probably receive a large bonus. Ownership that comes with decision making power, though, requires the vision to see where a business needs to go, the passion to take it there, the willingness to take calculated risks, the desire to see the business grow, and the ability to be part of the drive in that growth, including the leadership capabilities that are necessary. In a business, no matter how much a good employee says that they will leave if ownership is taken off the bargaining table, it is not advisable to give them decision-making power and owner status unless they possess ownership qualities.

The same is true when an owner leaves the business to his or her children. The current owner needs to assess the strengths of the potential owners as realistically and objectively as possible, whether these are family members or not. It may not seem fair to distribute or pass on the business according to strengths and weaknesses, but it is the right thing to do, taking into account all of the costs and benefits.

Let us say that all the children in a family are given ownership of the family business. Because some of them lack ownership strengths or the ability to "divvy up" decision making power according to each of their individual strengths, they argue about where the business needs to go, and some or all of them engage in habits or behavior patterns destructive to the business. In other words, only certain of them have the future vision and good business sense to be occupying "captain's and co-captain's chairs" on this boat. Fairness, as in "It's only fair to share the business with all the children," quickly becomes irrelevant as the business goes into failure mode. Therefore, even if all the children or "heirs to the throne" are to receive some ownership, the current owner needs to be cautious about which one of them becomes the managing partner and who among them is given decision making powers. In the end, even the person who right now thinks he or she wants ownership will be grateful not to have received something that he or she cannot handle, especially if they end up with less because they were trying to get more. My children are still of school age and I already have a very good idea of which one will be the managing partner of the family-owned business, should they decide to follow that path. Yes, I do want the other two to benefit from my life's work, but neither of them is of the right disposition or character to be the power person in the business. Not nice? Too bad, because in operating with Value Propositions, "nice" comes only as an accidental byproduct. Niceness is not an integral part of the Value Proposition process. And while the void left by the absence of niceness does not have to be filled with nastiness, the niceness sometimes needs to be put aside very deliberately so that the Value Proposition can serve its function. It is not a black-and-white choice of boxing gloves versus kid gloves, but something in between, like honest, down-to-business, gloveless hands-on.

What It Takes To Operate By Value Propositions

In Me, Inc or We, Inc, doing Value Propositions on relationships is not for the faint of heart. It requires a great deal of honest communication among all of your own departments and with your "prospects," the possible co-owners you may partner with. Obviously it will only work for those who want successful Win-Win relationships and not for those who want to manipulate or who have hidden agendas when entering into relationships. But when it is done with the right attitude and the right process, the end result – Priceless!

Choosing people with whom to enter into relationships and then attempting to engage them in the relationship can seem like selling to a prospect, but it is much more like exploring a possible co-ownership of a business with that person. I remember a line in the 1980 movie *The Competition*, with Amy Irving and Richard Dreyfus playing musicians who are competing with each other in a national competition. They develop a romantic relationship. On the night of the piano competition, Amy Irving's character wins and Richard Dreyfus' character places second. He is miffed and sour. She, however, is excited and says that it was like they are a corporation and the corporation has taken gold and silver. What a perfect "owner" thought! She puts the business first and assumes that everyone is doing the same. He will have nothing of it, though, and leaves her. The fact that he returns later can only be attributed to the corporate "home" she has created and the fact that he eventually "gets it."

There are many factors that need to be considered when choosing to become involved with someone. Of course, at this point in the book, I assume you know yourself and your departments. You also know your "relationship history." You know whether you have a tendency to choose healthy, productive relationships or destructive ones. If you stop and think, you know the signs of when you are about to "go over the edge." For example, there are certain people who feel at times like they have met their "soul mate," but who have had very bad experiences with people they thought were soul mates before. This pattern usually evolves because the repeat soul mate offenders are responding to cues programmed into them by their tribe. The person is mindlessly going along with a physical or emotional attraction that *seems* subconscious because they are not taking the time to examine the roots of the attraction. This person has probably systematically designed and packaged a product that attracts the very type of customer they should avoid. In fact the unmatched departments may be contributing to the destructive nature of the relationship. If you know that you have a history like this, when you feel that "soul mate" feeling, you should probably run the other way, or at least take things *very* slowly and thoughtfully.

It is very common for people to simply follow their initial attraction or to make their relationship decisions based on a single dimension or "benefit." For example, research has demonstrated a very strong positive relationship between the physical attractiveness ratings of married people. Overwhelmingly, attractive people tend to marry other attractive people. The attractive will say that it is just "accidental" and subconscious, or that "of course I noticed she was beautiful, but I based my decision to propose on her deeper qualities."

Naturally, we are preprogrammed to be attracted to people that our *global* tribe finds attractive. And it is difficult not to be indoctrinated into the attractiveness rules of our culture, especially now when people would need to be hermits in the woods to avoid the media that emphasizes beauty so much. Attractiveness is well defined in each culture and it is a powerful force. Attractive children are actually less likely to be "misplaced" in such ways as a parent walking away from them in a grocery store! We also all know that attractive people have advantages when it comes to being chosen for everything from teams to jobs. Unfortunately, though, if a person enters into a relationship because of physical attraction and does not stop to do a Value Proposition on this relationship as a whole, problems down the road are certainly being invited, if not inevitable. The same man who wants his wife to continue to be beautiful complains of the cost of facelifts and of being habitually late because "she takes two hours to dress!" He may even become dissatisfied with the lack of a deeper relationship.

Money is another benefit that tends to become a "deal maker." I have worked with many individuals who obviously made their relationship decision based on the other person's financial status. Here, the complaint ten years later may sound like, "I can never get his attention! He works constantly."

Most of the time, however, it takes quite a while before the "truths" come out. Many sessions into the coaching, the person or persons will realize and admit that the decision to become partners was based on one or two factors. A mindful, thorough Value Proposition process at the beginning of the relationship would have revealed this flawed thought process and possibly prevented the heartbreak that came later.

Years ago, on an episode of the gushy TV show *The Love Boat*, a woman made a "Pros and Cons" list about a man she was considering marrying. She came to the conclusion that if she needed the list, then she did not really want to marry him. I think she was wrong. The list was a great idea. If you *only* make lists and never go for a "test drive," then you are probably just sitting on the bleachers, but otherwise the lists, or our more sophisticated method of using the Decisional Balance Table, can come in very handy. I know many of you out there may see me as "objectifying" people and relationships. But after watching so many individuals, couples and families suffer the consequences of entering into the contract of a serious relationship without the benefit of Value Propositions, I see this as a much more human, and humane way to make such important life decisions.

With a healthy Value Proposition, a person might see that having come from a background of deprivation, he or she is naturally attracted to a mate who has a large "nest egg." A thoughtful person may see that having a beautiful mate makes him or her feel important, whereas feeling important should really be an "inside job." A person may see that having a powerful, aggressive mate is especially valued because of being bullied as a child. It would be obvious that marrying "just to get out of my parents' house" can be a disaster in the long run. Statements like, "He will make such a great father" would be deal breakers if there were not some others, such as "good partner," on the list also.

So what does it take to operate by Value Propositions? Certainly it takes an absence of hidden agendas and manipulation motives. If the relationship is to be more than shallow or temporary, then entering the relationship needs to be thought of as creating a co-owned business, *not* as a sales pitch to a prospect. Corporate thinking must transcend individual thinking. Just as a business must consider its own history and the history of prior similar businesses for guidance with how to proceed, so a person must explore what his or her personal and relationship histories tell the individual about the "hidden costs" of involvement with certain types of people. Finally, the Value Proposition thinker, to be successful, must be able to think along multiple dimensions, and must have the patience and take the time to gather the needed information. No whirlwind romances here!

Really Use The Value Proposition Idea

Of course, when there are two people involved, the *process* needs to involve two people. Find a retreat place where there are no distractions and spend some serious time first being sales people and prospects, but keeping the idea that your Me, Inc and the other Me, Inc may also become co-owners of a business, the newly formed We, Inc. Each of you gets the chance to talk about your own features and benefits and to hear what your potential partner sees as your features and benefits. With an upfront contract, there can be no hidden agendas and no surprises. This process can be powerfully productive, but be cautious and sensitive. Honesty of this magnitude can be difficult if not handled maturely and sensitively. Sometimes people have trouble seeing their own features, benefits and especially shortcomings. But if you have done your homework, you will each have a SWOT Analysis and possibly some Decisional Balance Tables, done on various topics, in your portfolios.

Each partner also gets the chance to see whether they like what their potential partner finds attractive. Some people may not want to be found attractive for the features that are listed. Maybe you do not want someone who focuses more on your power than on your kindness, for example. The rule of not living Life A and expecting Consequences B from the Goal Setting chapters is especially true when partnering. Some women are wildly attracted to a "tough" man who fights for her honor, but then these women are surprised when the tough man is not at all gentle. She initially found his jealousy, possessiveness and aggression toward other men flattering, but then at some point she becomes weary of the aggression, saying that it is embarrassing and obnoxious and that she would really like a man who talks about his feelings. Many men love their partners' humor and "wild" ways, but then become disappointed when life gets serious but the fun-loving partner does not. And many men are naturally drawn to sexy, "hot" partners, but do not want other men to notice (or be obvious about noticing) their partner's "augmentations." If you like a characteristic, accept the absence of its diametrically opposed, mutually exclusive opposite. Also make sure that you accept its "evil twin," or the downside that all upsides bring along. The tough man probably will not just be tough on guys who flirt with his partner, but is likely to get tough on his *partner*, too. Is it really unexpected when a man who likes to beat up other men turns on his wife or children? Or when the playful partner who cheated with you, later cheats on you? That is why the wedding vows say for better or worse, for richer or poorer and in sickness and in health. They could also say, "Yes, I will stay committed to this person while I am enjoying the benefits and the features I focused on, experiencing the disadvantages of those same features, and becoming aware of the absence of other features." Choosing people to inhabit our lives is not a process of "one from Column A, two from Column B."

Keep in mind also that during this process, you need to accept that what you see now is mostly what you will get in the future. Do not enter into this agreement assuming that there will be great changes. If there is something that you want changed, make clear what you want but hold off on the next level of commitment until you are convinced the change, if it occurs, is permanent. People only change when *they* are motivated, not when you desire them to change. Question: How many psychologists does it take to change a light bulb? Answer: Only one, but the light bulb has to want to be changed.

If both partners are happy with the Value Proposition and decide to move forward, then the next step is to create the corporation. The relationship becomes the business, the We, Inc. That means that another meeting is necessary to do a mission statement for We, Inc. Even if both partners are very happy with each other's products and they decide that the next step is to become co-owners, they must also be in agreement with how the company is going to proceed into the future. We might potentially be the best co-owners in the world together, but if you want to own an auto parts store and I want to run a sandwich shop, we are going to have problems. It is now time to find out if we have the same dreams and visions.

We may know that we are both Rainmakers, that we both have talents and ways of bringing happiness and productivity to the relationship, and that we both have owner potential, but can we sustain a business together? It is okay that we have different strengths and weaknesses, but they must be compatible. There are some universal talents needed to run a successful We, Inc together. Let's make sure that one of us has the ability to act under pressure but that somebody also knows how to check for all the details when we are contemplating an action. Let's make sure that we are not both going to suffer paralysis by analysis and that we are able to take action at some point. Let's make sure that one of us can "fire" the help when they do not perform well. If, for example, our mother/mother-in-law is not working out as a babysitter, or our old friend the accountant prepares our taxes poorly, can one of us, or both as a team, find a diplomatic but firm way to let the help go? Let's make sure that one of us has a really good Human Resources (HR) department and can create an employee handbook and "write up" the direct reports when they come up for evaluation. If neither one of us can make rules and discipline the children, then the company will be in trouble. Let's make sure that one of us has some bookkeeping knowledge and can come up with a balanced budget. Let's make sure that we agree on a company daycare policy and that we have some labor laws so nobody works so much that they have no life aside from the work.

But do not "sign" the contract until you like the whole "deal." Let's also make sure that each of us knows our own and our partner's strengths and that we defer to them when it is right to do so. In other words, can we put aside that evolutionarily built-in urge to be right when we need to for the good of the corporation? We need to promise not to grab things out of our partner's hands when they are the one who needs to be doing the job. Both of us need to be able to set aside our own desires when the company needs us. Wanting and striving for individual benefits is healthy, unless we forget that "the greater good" always comes first. We also need to plan for company growth, or not. If we both want the company to grow and expand, then what are our visions for when we become the "parent company?" Do we have compatible ideas and ideals for our "spinoffs?"

What About The "Already" Relationships?

The above advice is great for those relationship contracts, or We, Incs, that have not been signed into existence yet. What about those contracts that are already gathering dust? It may be time to bring them out, wipe them off and re-evaluate each of them. Value Propositions need to be done on each of the contracts that your Me, Inc is involved in. The real value of a Value Proposition for We, Incs is twofold: First, it can help to determine which relationships are "too far gone" to be saved, the ones that need to be ended. Second, it can light up the "what needs to be changed and fixed" button in the relationships that are going to be retained. The Value Proposition process is the same as always. Make lists and use the Decisional Balance Table. Knowing the Pros and Cons of the current status will come in very handy, as will estimating the Pros and Cons of the "changed" relationship, whether the change is to end or to "tune up."

Of course, you will need to be brutally honest with yourself when it comes to "What am I getting paid to stay in this relationship?" For some of you who are in unhealthy relationships, this may include benefits such as liking someone else dependent on you, enjoying being worshiped, enjoying having a "whipping" person, not wanting to be "out there" alone, feeling that you must settle because you are not worthy of having any better, being too scared to make any change, feeling obligated, needing to be needed even if it is by someone who is destructive, being addicted to a person as if that person is a substance, or liking the money or status that being with the person affords you.

When it comes to making decisions about family of origin relationships, keep in mind that while it is not politically correct to end these We, Incs, sometimes it is necessary. Many people frown on broken families of origin. It may be because they have wanted to terminate a relationship and just "could not," or that they have some family-implanted, ingrained beliefs that make the termination a taboo. If you go in the direction of terminating a relationship with a parent, sibling, or more distant family member, make sure that you are very honest with yourself about assessing the real location of the toxicity. If it is really you causing the problems, and not the allegedly toxic family member, then get some help. Help-seeking is good to consider at a time like this, anyway. Finding the strength even to consider breaking a family tie, let alone actually making the break, is often painful and difficult. It takes courage to proactively end any relationship. Most of the time people just let relationships fall into disrepair and end by default. While this may seem like the easiest way, it also has a very disempowering effect and keeps the parties involved feeling like they are in limbo. It perpetuates unhealthy communication habits.

Remember in Box C of the Decisional Balance table, the Pros of the Current State, we often need to look at some ugly truths about what is driving us to stay the way we are or where we are. I have dealt many times with people who could not handle the guilt they believed they would feel if they stopped enabling someone else's bad behavior. This is especially common with parents who have children who are addicted or emotionally unstable. Even after the Value Proposition shows that the benefit of maintaining the relationship's status quo is minimal and the destructive costs are extreme, mothers especially have a tough time changing the contract of the relationship. A common excuse might sound like, "He's been through so much, he just needs this crutch a little longer, " or "I'm terrified what will happen to her if I stop doing what I have been doing." Another, often father's-side equivalent is when a child is on track to follow in his or her father's successful footsteps, but the child is clearly miserable stepping in those footsteps. As with addiction, the father may be enabling the offspring's unhappy behavior, by pushing his child to stay on the path the father wishes, or by creating "opportunities" for the child that the child looks at with guilt-ridden dread. We may hear such fathers say, "Just go to this one more interview with my friend in the Admissions Office. Then if you still don't want medical school, I'll let it go." Or either parent may be heard to use the all-purpose, dripping-with-guilt line, "I just want the best for you," but in reality they should follow up with "as long as it conforms to what will make *me* happy." Often times, however, when such parents do succeed in changing their own behavior and changing what they are willing to "pay" their child, so that their own Me, Inc becomes bearable again, the child's life changes dramatically for the better, too. Of course this is because the child is now being paid for different behaviors and the We, Inc has morphed into a whole new company.

Company Policies

Finally, for both relationships that are forming and for those that are ready for an overhaul, address "Company Policies." There needs to be a Code of Conduct in relationship corporations just as in any corporation. First and foremost, just as with Me, Inc, the We Inc must have a good Sales Department. We, Inc must agree to present a united, positive front. This means that you never "dis" your partner to anyone. If you have a genuine problem with your partner, and cannot solve it between the two of you, then you are called upon to seek out the help of someone who wants you to succeed and who cares about you. This may be a professional or a trusted friend who you know has the interests of both of you equally at heart. No, this will not generally be someone from either of your families of origin! There is only so far unemotional objectivity can extend, and it usually ends at the family boundaries.

A thorough set of company policies will also address complaining. Pointless complaining just fuels the bad blood. If you catch yourself complaining with someone about your partner, remind yourself that you are just triangulating and that it is like taking a drug. Also remind yourself that you are part of We, Inc, and keep in mind that when you are in a relation-*ship*, whenever you take shots at your partner, or anyone in the corporation, you are "shooting holes in your own boat." The best advice here is to be honest and accountable. If you are *not* going to do something constructive to solve a problem, then "shut up." It is poisonous and destructive on so many levels to talk negatively about your business partner. In Chapter 2, I discussed how outsiders view a company when the Sales Department or other employees talk negatively about the company. Imagine how people view a company when one of the *owners* is talking negatively about another owner. Positive thinking and talking are much more likely to produce positive results. Negative talk will most likely lead to negative actions and will certainly at least bring you down and drive a wedge between you and your partner. It is also sad and scary to watch the effects of destructive words and actions on the employees of We, Inc. When I work with couples, if they are going to stay together and try to work on the relationship, I forbid any negative talk. There is a very big difference between stating a problem and talking negatively. In general, problem statements will be "I" or "We" statements or will have a "we" tone to them. They might be such statements as, "I feel badly about the way our son spoke to us this morning," or "We seem to have a problem moving from diagnosing a problem to acting on a solution." Talking negatively, however, typically involves, "you" or "he/she" statements, negatively toned pronouncements about what is wrong with your/his/her behavior. The worst forms, of course, are assaults on another person's character. Examples might include, "You always hoard the best stuff for yourself. You are stingy!", "Joey just lies, lies, lies! I am ashamed to call him my stepson," or "You never can take into account anyone else's point of view but your own. I've been reading about this issue online. You are a narcissist!"

The "positive thinking and no negative talk" rule transfers to your direct reports, the children, as well. Your HR department can confront and "write up" the employee and can even call in professional help. You cannot, however, say negative things about your employees to others. Your Sales and Advertising department cannot be putting out negative information about the company. If that department is getting these urges, then there is a problem. Under these circumstances, I always encourage my clients to ask themselves "What can *I* do to make things better" or "What can *I* do differently that might help?" This question is always better than asking or complaining about what someone else could do differently.

When To Use Mirrors, When To Use Windows?

It has been said that a great leader looks in the mirror when things go wrong. In other words, when there is a problem, he or she looks at what he or she is doing. When things are good, that same great leader looks out the window. In other words, during successful times, he or she looks at the business partners and the direct reports and others responsible and says, "We did a great job." Such leaders know they need to be the driving force and that they need to lead by modeling. What others can do is of little importance, since even great leaders cannot change other people. There is almost always something we can do differently, even if it is just to be happy. If you are being negative and behaving badly, then what is the difference what your partner is doing wrong? Create the best environment possible and do not contribute to the negativity. You can then better see what the real problems are. Some of them may disappear. In fact, people who refuse to be affected by negativity around them and who maintain a positive attitude are more likely to be rewarded by seeing other people coming over to their side. Pollyanna, from the Disney movie by that name, may have been accused of being unrealistic, but she was always happy and most of the people around her were hard pressed to remain cynical or negative once she blessed them with her positive words of wisdom.

Since there is never a guarantee about the outcome of a relationship, I can only encourage people to look at themselves when entering into coaching. Coaching or counseling is best sought for the sake of the person entering into it. But no matter what happens to the relationship, if a person becomes the best he or she can be, even if they end up out on their own, no harm, no foul. And especially when both partners of a We, Inc, *acting as individuals on their own behalf,* are following the Rules of Engagement and living "no matter what," there are worlds to be gained.

It is always easier to save a We, Inc that does not have an escape clause. And while dissolution of a We, Inc should not be impossible, it seems to me that today, relationships are far too easily and casually ended. It is understandable that people want happiness and life satisfaction. In my work with couples, however, I see far too many people so busy scrambling and "fighting," not for the team but for their own desires. They are forgetting that their first obligation is to create a We, Inc environment that is safe and peaceful for the "employees," the direct reports, that they hired. It is possible for co-owners to work toward a better tomorrow while keeping a good today. Rocking the relation-***ship*** may be necessary for growth, but filling it full of holes or capsizing it just drowns everyone.

Some Bad Communication Habits
That Indicate Problems In Relationships

It is important to stop and analyze when communication warning flags come up in a relationship. For example, if someone is speaking harshly and they are not in any *real* danger, the harsh words are their own choosing. Any of the traditional "buts," such as "but I told her that already," or "but he doesn't listen to me," or "but I'm right," should be ignored. These buts can be answered with the following in a questioning tone: "I'm hearing you say that you are having trouble managing your frustration?" If a person is receiving feedback from a person who *genuinely cares*, and the receiver is being defensive, then that receiver needs to check out their Customer Service Department. Good feedback should be answered with, "Thank you. I will look into that," just as a good Customer Service rep in a business would. Being thankful for people who give us caring "360's" is smart business management.

If a person is responding to another person's communication attempts with silence and withdrawing, what is called "stonewalling," then all parties involved in the process need to be assessed. Stonewalling is a fear response. This means that the communication process does not feel safe. There may be some overreacting on the part of the "stonewaller," or maybe the other person or people are actually being scary. Check it out carefully.

Finally, when a person is using disgust and contempt in their communication, it is way out of bounds and the other players need to clear the field. Much of the time, contempt is a sign of such low self-esteem that the person needs to reach for the cheapest and easiest method of putting someone else down. Regardless of what the contemptuous person wants to portray, it is a universal sign of hatred to the person on the receiving end. Contempt should not be tolerated. In fact, John Gottman, a researcher who has devoted much of his life to studying relationships in scientifically exacting ways, has found that when contempt shows up in the dialogue between couples, there is a 95 per cent chance that the relationship will not "make it."

Upfront Contracts, With The Emphasis On "Upfront"

The generation that is now in their 20s has coined a new expression, "friends with benefits." This means that the relationship is in the "only friends" category, but has sexual benefits. This type of promiscuous behavior has occurred in many points in history, and as recently as the "hippie" generation was called "free love." Interestingly, when benefited friends from the past show up to meet new lovers or mates, the same type of jealousy and suspicion is there that was always there when "ex's" showed up. In other words, the introduction of sex into the relationship carried it to a level beyond "friend," *as it naturally does.* And for the most part, people still end up mating with one other person and infidelity is still something that makes partners feel betrayed and they often end up splitting over.

I am realistic, however, and I know that whatever my opinions may be, the definition and parameters of a relationship are completely up to the individuals involved. All that I suggest is to make clear what "my way" is. Before advancing to any next step, the meaning of that step, and the means by which it will be done, need to be made clear to everyone involved. Different choices might be made if advancing a friendship to the "benefits" stage is taken totally casually by one partner while the other partner is secretly hoping for a committed, monogamous relationship. I always recommend that people not fool themselves or any of the other people involved in the contract.

Take it a step further. If there is any possibility that the encounter can result in a new "direct report," no matter what birth control you are using, you need to have a plan in place for the "possibilities." I also strongly suggest that you have some serious talks about your beliefs in this area, upfront contract-style. Look long and hard at your partner, because with today's laws and mores, if you "accidentally" have a child, the other parent will be in your life for a long time. And the "in your life" may not be a good time. In my business, I get to see people from the whole spectrum of "children beliefs." I watch people torment over their children being in the hands of a partner they have come to perceive as pure evil. I have watched while children opt to "go with" a parent who is cruel. And mean people learn very quickly how to use their children as a weapon against the other partner. It is quite awful to see that in some broken relationships, both partners engage in this behavior. If you do not know a person's Me, Inc policies on employees, keep yourself dressed and start *thinking* with another part of your anatomy.

Upfront contracts change the face of all relationships. There are *universals* in body language and some behaviors, such as smiles, raised fists and disgusted looks. But once we are beyond the superficial parts of a relationship, we apply individual cognitive evaluations. In other words, each of us starts to assign our own meanings to our own and our partners' behaviors. These behaviors are redefined and are perceived in a new light. With upfront contracts, there is no room for doubt. They give vital information about a person's values and beliefs. Asking questions about what a behavior or phrase means to the people in a We, Inc is a good sign that you are taking a proactive stance on your partnering. If the other person does not like to be questioned, then you start to see very soon that they are probably not your "We" type. This dislike of explanations and sharing information may indicate that the other person does not want to *share power* in their We, Incs. Sharing power involves assertive communication versus aggressive communication, willingness to compromise, mutual disclosure of feelings, willingness to "back off" when your partner is feeling pressured, equal financial freedom, and explanations of motives for behaviors. In my work with couples and business partners, I have found that the unwillingness of partners to share power with each other is the most common reason that partnerships dissolve. Dissolution of partnerships almost always comes at extreme costs to the partners and to innocent bystanders. Value Propositions and Upfront Contracts possibly could have stopped many of these partnerships from forming before they did the damage. But if everyone becomes the best that they can be, then using these tools can help prevent destruction even in some difficult relationships that stay intact.

Chapter 9

CEO Roundtables and Masterminds: Support Systems For The You Business

They're your CEO experts and they sit in the round.
When you're in trouble they are there to expound.
They know all there is about you and your biz,
So when there is strife they'll be there in a whiz.

When there's only one set of prints in the sand,
You'll know it's not you and your one man band.
The CEO Rounds are there for you to lean,
Carrying you high and keeping you clean.

So lean on them hard when you need the extra mile,
But thank and praise them 'cause to stay they need your smile.
If you keep them well tended they'll continue to grow
And the bottom line profits of Me, Inc. will show.

The Plain White Rapper

Great leaders, or owners, know that they cannot do it all. They know that they have limitations and they know that there is nothing worse than a closed, stagnant system. They also know that even the strongest people have setbacks and stumbles. These great leaders want input from others and they want support when times are tough.

If the great leader is in a large corporation or business, then he or she has a Board of Directors. The purpose of the Board is to make executive decisions and to see to it that the business is kept on its true course. It is up to the Board to see to it that the company continues in the direction of its mission and vision. An ideal Board believes in the company and yes, loves the company. Therefore, the company can trust that all ideas will be given and decisions will be made in its best interest.

Small companies have the same needs that large companies have, just on a smaller scale. For them, there are CEO (Chief Executive Officer) Roundtables that serve some of the functions of a Board of Directors. These groups are systematically assembled by the owner or owners of the small business. They consist of people who are genuinely interested in the success of the business and who want to give some of their time either at a reduced rate or for no fee. Many times a CEO Roundtable is made up of people from different professions who serve as advisors to the small business. There may be an accountant, an attorney, a marketing executive, a human resource person, or just other people who are business owners. The group is formed based on what the owner or owners need for input and support. Many of these people benefit from the success of the business because they are vendors to that business, or their business improves when the core business improves. For example, if the restaurant next door to my arcade is very busy, then my arcade gets overflow business from the restaurant, and vice versa. The restaurant owner and I might consider being part of each other's CEO Roundtable. When used correctly, all of the consultants to a business become part of the CEO Roundtable to that business. An attorney and an accountant lend valuable knowledge, advice and technical skill to the small business owner who knows when to bring others into the circle. She understands that the money for this type of consulting is well spent because relying on her own skills in areas where she is untrained would be far more expensive than the consulting fees. Once a small business owner has established a relationship with consultants, many questions can be answered in a casual manner without the consultant being officially "on the clock." And then when there is a larger issue, the small business owner has the professional available on a per hour billable basis. Both parties benefit from this relationship.

Another type of support system that many small business owners and solo practitioners use is the Mastermind Group. It usually consists of a small group of people who are all in the same general "industry," but who are not competing for the same target market. In other words they usually specialize in different areas, such as a contractor who works only on commercial properties and a contractor who works only on residential properties. The members of Masterminds are sometimes all geographically close to each other or they may be scattered and choose an agreed upon location for their meetings. While CEO Roundtables are usually more useful for the day to day "grind" of the business, a Mastermind Group can be very helpful for setting goals and for those times when the business owner wants to grow the business or achieve a specific goal. Masterminds meet anywhere from monthly to quarterly. All that I have heard of have very strict guidelines about commitment. If someone cannot consistently make the meetings, they are asked to leave. Of course, this is an Upfront Contract at the time the group is started. There is an agenda and each person has time to present their issues. The point is to give and receive feedback in a safe environment, because, of course, what happens in the Mastermind stays in the Mastermind.

Types of Support For Me, Inc.

Since all businesses have some type of support system, naturally your Me, Inc will need a support system. A good support system does not just happen accidentally. It takes maintenance and care. Just as in any other business, Me, Inc needs to match up the issue with the support person needed, just as a business takes a tax problem to a tax accountant or tax attorney. Take some time to check out your support systems and carefully read the guidelines in Figures 9.1 and 9.2.

Figure 9.1
Types Of Needs and Human Support

CORE PEOPLE NEEDS

Safety: Supplied by people with whom we feel emotionally secure sharing "anything," because they don't judge us, and those with whom we can share our hopes, dreams, fears, tragedies, and vulnerabilities.

Empathy: Supplied by people who sense our feelings, thoughts, and questions about life, sometimes even before we speak them; who are courageous enough to ask us about, or to state outright, what they sense; who urge us to be true to ourselves and guide us to see ourselves and the world in new ways; and who help us value our experience and find our strengths and inner courage.

Cutting to the Chase: Supplied by people who are caring and assertive enough to tell us, gently if possible, but firmly if needed, when we are behaving unwisely, self-destructively, or in violation of our principles and values.

NOTE: Our best, most prized support suppliers probably combine all three of the above – safety, understanding, and directness. Are you fortunate enough to have one or more people that are in all three categories above? Are you a person who provides all three to anyone in your life? "We get as good as we give."

ADDITIONAL PEOPLE NEEDS

Tenderness and Affection: Supplied by people who are gentle and who share physical affection easily.

Health Promotion: Supplied by people who encourage healthy habits; who make us aware of our bodies and their value without creating negative self-consciousness; and who confront us when we are failing to tend to our health (see also Cutting to the Chase).

Mental Stretching: Supplied by people who are knowledgeable; who point out new facts and ideas; who encourage and stimulate learning and thinking; and who urge us to use our intellect in new ways.

Figure 9.2
Inner and Non-Human Supports

INNER SUPPORTS

These are our key internal resources. They can be used when support from people is not readily available. One or both of them, however, are especially powerful when used in combination with good safety, empathy, and directness from others.

Beliefs, Ideals, and Principles: These represent what we stand for and value most highly. They are the ideas that are strong and widely influential enough to provide vision and purpose in our lives; to guide our choices and actions; and to keep us afloat in times of confusion and difficulty.

Memories: The most grounded, real, accessible learnings are those that are already in our experience. We access this storehouse by asking ourselves, "What does my experience tell me to think or do here? When and where and how have I been successful handling similar challenges?" The memories we access may be instances of problem-solving, the echoes of words of wisdom, or simply pleasurable experiences the recalling of which give us some relaxation and serenity.

Example: The memory of when I did well debating my history teacher. This memory helps me recognize the sharpness of my intellect, when I make a point of believing in myself.

CONDUITS:

Conduits are called this because they are best used as channels to connect us with our inner supports. While they may be of some temporary comfort in times of need, conduits should not be used to the exclusion of people-based supports or the accessing of inner resources. Conduits include:

- Special "life forms" such as pets, plants, wildlife or stuffed animals.
- Meaningful activities such as journaling, meditation, listening to music, reading, attending worship, or a regularly scheduled celebration, picnic, family reunion, etc.
- Special objects such as pictures, souvenirs, or charms.
- Special places such as favorite rooms or chairs, spots in nature and other "sanctuaries."

Look at your life closely. Does your Me, Inc have people that serve each of the functions in Figure 9.1? If not, do some work on putting together a team. Looking only in the mirror all of the time can give us a very narrow view of the world and of ourselves. As discussed in Chapter 3, we all need love, we all need touch and we all need to be listened to and understood while feeling emotionally safe. People in the Safety, Empathy and Tenderness and Affection categories above provide for these basic belonging-related needs. We also all need to grow and to be challenged at times. And something that can be very hard to get is a support person who will honestly tell you when you are wrong. This does not mean people who will make fun or just criticize. This means a person or people who genuinely care about you, but who will risk your anger or disapproval by telling you the truth. People in the Cutting to the Chase, Health Promotion and Mental Stretching categories take care of the growth and challenge needs.

Going To The Right Places

Just as it would be a huge mistake for the small business owner to go to his attorney when a plumber was needed, it is a mistake for Me, Inc to reach for the wrong type of support in the Life Business. Look around at your life and the lives of those you know. Have you ever watched someone crash and burn because they chose the wrong person to "hang out" with at the wrong time? For example, imagine a woman whose marriage is shaky starting to hang out with a group of resentful divorcees who go out, get drunk, bash men and behave promiscuously. Imagine a man who is grieving the loss of his wife spending a lot of time with several other men who have never moved on from a loss.

When children have life-changing announcements to make, they need a parent who will be supportive and understanding, even if the parent does not like the news or agree with the choice. First and foremost, they need for everyone to follow the *Rules Of Engagement* and to listen. And then any disagreement needs to be kept in an arena that is tolerable for all of the partners of We, Inc. We are all programmed to rebel and test our wings some. A healthy tribe encourages individuality and careful risk taking, while setting boundaries. This creates an environment conducive to creativity and self-esteem, but also helps to develop individuals who respect rules. Keep in mind that if the tribe we are born into is harsh and disapproving of us, we find another tribe where we can belong. Many times when teenagers behave destructively, they are rebelling against a tribe where they felt "wrong" or they are hanging with a tribe full of others in the same boat who "like me the way I am."

Acts of reaching out to support systems can become defining

moments for children and for adults. Rejection when one really needs a supporting word or hug can sting for a long time. Conversely, being embraced and listened to with comforting, supportive words and touch can change your life. On the other hand, support can sometimes be too soft. If you are neglecting your health, treating key people poorly, or headed on a course to disaster personally or in business, you need not only safety and understanding, but someone who will say, "Your marriage boat is about to crash on the rocks" or "Your anger is causing the people in your life to go away."

While the quality of the support system is very important, another issue that can come up is about quantity. If most of your types of support come from one person such as a spouse or a very dear friend, and that one person wears too many hats, your team may be in trouble. It is not that you are failing to get the support that you need, it is just that your team lacks depth, like a football team with only one quarterback. If you lose that one person, then you will be absent some crucial support. So if your team is a bit shallow, consider doing some recruiting for Me, Inc. There are billions of people out there in the world. Certainly some of them are qualified players for your Me, Inc team.

Unaccessed Support Is No Support At All

No matter what type of CEO Roundtable or Mastermind group a business owner has, it will have no effect if he or she never consults them. While meetings can be frivolous and sometimes an excuse to do nothing, they are also critical to giving and receiving support. Me, Inc must actually reach out to the people that serve as your support system or they can do you no good. Yes, sometimes it is difficult to reach out. At times we feel embarrassed by what is bothering us or by what we consider a failure. But looking good and hiding the truth does not solve problems. These times are when the Sales and Production Departments must really match.

Find a way to dispense with the very common excuse not to access your support system of "I don't want to be a burden." If this is something you find yourself saying, then ask yourself, first, would you be there for them without feeling burdened? If not, then true, asking for their support could be asking for something you are not willing to give, which is a one-sided, having-your-cake-and-eating-it-too arrangement. If, however, you are there for your people but they feel that you are a burden, then ask yourself why you are hanging with people who do not want reciprocal relationships. This question will take you right back to Chapter 8 idea of basing your relationships on Value Propositions.

Finally, we all know that we cannot be there for everyone all the time. You need, however, to give yourself the right to ask for support when you need it. It is not your job to "second guess" everyone in your circle. Sometimes, some of your support people are going to be tied up with other obligations or in the midst of their own messes. *It is up to them* to say, "Sorry, I cannot help right now" if they are too busy or indisposed. Give them the normal adult responsibility of being assertive. Each of us is responsible to pay the price if we say "Yes" when we really mean "No."

Problem-Solving

One of the main functions of the CEO Roundtables and the Masterminds is to solve problems. But the process of problem-solving involves some very distinct steps combined with "out of the box" thinking. Ignoring problems or faulty problem-solving can be very costly to a business. It would be far too optimistic to say that all companies, especially those with Boards of Directors, CEO Roundtables and other supports, solve problems skillfully and well. Unfortunately, businesses are at the behest of those individuals at the helm. And those individuals are not all wonderful problem solvers, nor are they all wise enough to know when they need help with problem-solving. In fact, in my business consulting, I can say that many times when a business fails or falters, it is due to the person at the helm not wanting to give up enough control to admit to needing help.

Faulty or absent problem-solving exists partly because in the midst of our focus on academic subjects, we do not really teach emotional intelligence, knowing our limitations, or how to solve problems, especially human ones. There are, however, very specific tactics involved in problem-solving that good businesses engage in. For example, imagine that you are the manager of a department store and one day you stand outside of your store and you see customers not being attended to and leaving the store empty handed. An uneducated manager may go out and immediately hire new people thinking that the sales staff is not handling the volume. But then he or she watches as the sales staff stands around most of the time because the "rush" was only on Thursdays when the restaurant next door had their dinner special and their customers shopped before and after. Or, consider the "team building activity" of having pairs of people stand on opposite sides of a line, with the assignment to "get your opponent on the same side of the line as you are on." Many pairs try to "win," so they argue, persuade and try to convince the other person to "come over to my side." The simple solution is to step over the line to where your "opponent" is standing. *Voila!* You are both on the same side of the line.

Problem-solving requires some scientific knowledge, but mostly common sense, open-mindedness and good observation skills. Once again, the whys are usually the issue when problem-solving is not approached intelligently. When people become frustrated with a problem because there is no solution or the solution is extremely complex and difficult, or because they cannot carry out the solution, they sometimes fall into the fallacy of solving any other convenient problem or throwing money at the actual problem. There is a joke about a man looking under a street light for something he has lost. The man explains that he lost the object somewhere else, but when asked why he is looking in this spot, he responds, "There is light here." Funny, but not so fictional. I believe that "just solving" is what many schools have done in response to the school shootings. Look at the facts. Virtually all of the school shootings have been "inside jobs," done by students. Yet the response has been to lock the school down and make the parents get "buzzed in." If there is violence, the students are locked into their classrooms to wait, even though the gunmen are probably insiders who know the whole "Crisis Plan" and will not be fooled by the dark, quiet classrooms.

On the way home from my twin boys' school there is a fast food restaurant. As a special treat during the warm weather, I occasionally allowed them to stop in on their way home from school. They reported to me near the end of the last school year that when school children misbehaved, the manager would speak to them about it and would sometimes, after severe misbehavior, make the misbehavers leave. At the beginning of this year, when my sons went into the restaurant, they were told they could not get served without an adult present because of the kids that come in and cause trouble. Very misguided problem-solving! My boys were good customers and they behaved well, enjoying their meal and the "big boy" time this afforded them. Rather than identifying the trouble makers, the management used random discipline, did not follow through on the discipline, then became restrictive at everyone's expense, *including their own.* Now we will never go back to that restaurant again, and "word-of-mouth" is not favorable about a business that tries to solve its problems in such a scattershot, one-size-fits-all fashion.

Problem-solving in a Me, Inc or We, Inc business can have many of the same issues as in other businesses. For example, when there is a behavior problem in a family member, an efficient problem-solving approach would be to first define the problem in terms of visible behavior so that everyone involved knows exactly what the problem is. Next, measure the problem behavior. The type of measurement, whether it is frequency, duration or intensity, will depend upon the particular behavior. Especially when there is more than one person involved, it is important to measure or "chart" the behavior you are interested in changing. In our household, one of my husband's jobs in the morning is to open the blinds. This is because arthritis in my hands makes this job difficult for me. For a brief period of time he was forgetting this job. When confronted with the issue, he claimed that it was very rare that he forget. I, of course, saw the situation differently. As it turned out, all that was needed was for me to threaten charting and it has become a family joke. As he opens the blinds in the morning, he exclaims, "I don't want to get charted!" This example demonstrates in the extreme what behaviorists know, that whenever a behavior is measured, it improves an average of 20%, and often much more, just by being attended to. The improvement increases as you add emotional intelligence and motivation. Emotional intelligence is quite different from academic intelligence. It involves abilities such as delaying gratification and reading other peoples' tones and body language. Emotional intelligence also includes knowing how to "pick your fights," standing your ground when it is important and deferring to others' wishes when that is the wiser course. My husband knows I am serious about my need to have him open the blinds, because he reads my tones and postures correctly. He usually picks his fights well, and in this case, he knows my medical condition is disabling in certain ways. He is willing to take it into account, instead of arguing for his own cause, even when he is in a hurry to get to the office in the morning. He has done his cost-benefit analysis on this issue. These are the ingredients for the emotional intelligence recipe! An example of combining emotional intelligence and motivational factors is to focus on *desired behavior and positive consequences* more than on undesired behavior and punishment. Even though my husband's blind-opening behavior is a very "lightweight" example, it is easy to translate to almost any problem in Me, Inc, whether it be swearing, drinking, working too many hours, spending money or speaking harshly. Just keep in mind that you must use behavioral language so that all parties know what is being discussed and use measurement *in the moment* instead of "I just know you do that all the time."

In working with the Me and We, Incs, though, much of the time what I see is people raging or complaining, rather than systematically solving problems. So of course the question I confront them with becomes, "What do you want more than a solution?" Upon closer examination, the answer is usually that complaining and blaming is easy while solutions are hard work. Sometimes, though, people are seeking to be listened to about their issue and then they are more receptive to working for real solutions. We cannot underestimate the value of "validation" when someone is having a problem.

Problem-solving is just taking all of the concepts we have already covered and applying them to a specific situation. In order to solve the problem, the people involved must be able to communicate and to be honest about all of their motivations. They must be capable of understanding all of the whys involved before they attempt the hows. And most of all, they must be able to handle the costs involved in problem-solving. People who believe that they can "have it all" are at a distinct disadvantage for getting the issues resolved. When there is a fork in the road, you cannot take both paths. Problem-solving requires the ability to make decisions and to take some risks. Especially when it comes to We, Inc, the "owners" must take a leap of faith. I turn couples away when one partner is not sure about staying in the relationship. It is amazing to see how petty fighting and complaining are transformed to commitment when both partners start working with "no matter what" attitudes. Little "no matter whats" are situational, as in "No matter what, we will *not* go to bed angry tonight." The biggest "no matter what" is, "We will make this work and be happy together, no matter what."

Use Your Supports The Right Way

The most significant factor that separates people who come through disasters intact, from people who are traumatized or who go through a physical or mental breakdown, is the presence of good support systems. Because some people affected by the disaster will lack good support systems, trauma teams, including people just to function as supports, are now sent to disaster sites. In addition, any seasoned counselor or coach knows that although clients present themselves for treatment by saying they are looking for help with depression, addictive habits and similar afflictions, when it comes right down to it, they are also looking for support and "someone to talk to" that they do not have in their everyday lives. The title of the 1964 book by William Schofield which was popular among counselors recognized this by calling psychotherapy "the purchase of friendship."

I can tell you to build a good support system, and this chapter has shown the elements that go into it. I can tell you to access that support system, and use it for problem-solving and to avoid using it for whining, "blowing off steam" or complaining. And I can tell you to be wise in choosing the right places to go for support. But we live in a social world and are naturally social beings. What is more, we have evolutionarily programmed needs to belong and to be listened to and understood. These facts make much of what we advise people to do regarding their support systems merely common sense and something that we are naturally prepared to do. So if your support systems are poor, lacking or not functioning well, then we must sound that by-now-familiar theme: Do what you can with the how-to advice in this chapter, but there will probably be some important whys that you will need to answer when it comes to fixing this issue.

Chapter 10

The Wrap Up: Conclusions

The Wrap It Up Rap

You have successfully completed the course on *CLO*,
But still you're not quite ready to leave and go.
Stay for just a minute for the final Wrap Rap
And then you can gather up your Me, Inc map.

If you think the wrap chap is just a throwaway,
As in the intro rap, I urge you to stay.
Slow down and we can help you tie up loose ends,
Then all the business talk will become your own trends.

There's lots of ground we've covered, go ahead and re-read,
Because the most important thing is getting up to speed.
It sounds ironic, but to get your speed, go slow.
Take the time to know how much you've really come to know.

The Plain White Rapper

Soon it will be "That's a wrap!" for *CLO*. I would like to present
you with a summary of the material to which you have been exposed.
Along with this, I would like to offer you a suggestion or two of what
you can do if you find yourself short of knowledge, confidence or skill
in applying the lessons in any of the areas listed.

- In the first chapter, I introduce *CLO*'s guiding metaphor, the idea of life as a business. I ask you to bring an open mind, in both the sense of being receptive to the ideas and open in the sense of being willing to apply yourself to the ideas. Since action and teaching others are the two best ways to learn, I suggest that you work the concepts by deliberately thinking in terms of them, passing them along to others, and most of all doing recommended exercises and *behaving in some new ways* in line with new ideas.

- In the second chapter, "Only Sell What You Produce", on your Departments, or the parts of yourself that need to work together to make life successful, I talk about Production, what your Self actually does and puts out into the world. Under this is stressed the need for self-knowledge, especially about your strengths. Under Human Resources, I address self-caretaking. Me, Inc's Research and Development Department is that part responsible for your growth and self-improvement, without which life becomes stagnant and starts to move backwards. Marketing and Sales has to do with what you broadcast to the world about yourself, and there, I emphasize the need for truthful but positive self-talk and projections to others. A major point is made of the critical importance of having your Production and Sales departments in harmony, not tearing you apart by telling the world that you are one thing while actually being something else. And I emphasize that life is not lived well or in a healthy fashion if you are the Emperor, going naked in the world but insisting that everyone tell you how beautiful your new clothes are. The themes that run through the Departments chapter are those of self-care and growth, authenticity and self-awareness, in the large sense of knowing yourself in general and the equally important sense of being aware of your experience in the moment.

- The third chapter, "SWOT First, Plan Next", covers making a business plan for Me, Inc, based on a soul-searching exploration of your Strengths, Weaknesses, Opportunities and Threats (SWOT). The three keys to a good SWOT

Analysis are honesty, a broad view of yourself and your life at present, and *to do it!* You may have been able to bring yourself to do the SWOT analysis, but perhaps you have done it alone, or you feel that it is missing certain parts or points, or you think that your SWOT Analysis is biased, that you were excessively kind or harsh on yourself. If any of these apply, get with some people who know you well and who have the broad, unbiased view of you and your life that you are having trouble getting.

- In "To Do Or Not To Do: Goal-Setting Part 1," I set out a portrayal of our evolution which led to our foremost human needs being *to belong* and *to be listened to and understood.* Humans strive to obtain More and to avoid pain, and can be easily overtaken by such basic reinforcers as food. I also put forth the idea that above and beyond More, pain avoidance and simple animal rewards, the striving for Mastery is also a natural human drive. There are two major sticking points that can be trouble for most of us which can be easily understood from the model of human nature in this chapter. First, the environment may not provide us with a sufficient sense of belonging or being understood. If this was true earlier in our life, it may persist and we may continue to see the world in terms of beliefs such as "I will never get my needs met, no matter how I try." The second sticking point is that people can become *immersed* in seeking More, in pain avoidance or in basic reinforcers to an overwhelming degree. This can lead to being engaged in addictive or compulsive behavior to such an extent that they do not have enough left to invest in their Mastery strivings. They may even be unaware of the possibility of a Mastery-driven life.

  If you find either of these is the case with you, seek to be as mindful as you can be and record when you are responding to feeling the need for More, the need to avoid pain, or the need to engage in your own forms of "substance abuse." This mindfulness will give you the whys and set you up for the next chapter.

- In "Ready, Set, Goal: Goal-Setting Part 2," I introduce the

151

Decisional Balance Table. It is used to determine whether your motives for making a change or setting out toward a goal are adequate to motivate the change effort and to enable you to face and surmount any obstacles that are likely. A strong Decisional Balance picture is one in which a person: perceives the negative consequences of remaining the same; can foresee some positive consequences to the change once it is completed; does not see too many "goodies" coming from the present, unchanged state; and does not see too many aversive or challenging consequences coming from the changed state.

The Decisional Balance approach is quite a detailed one. A common glitch is that at the moment we are contemplating a certain change, we may only be able to see the negative outcomes of our present behavior, but we lack any positive motives. That is, we cannot at this point foresee the upside of the changed state. It is difficult to maintain a change when all we have to motivate us are "the monsters nipping at our heels," and we fail to see anything good up ahead once we outrun the monsters. For this, I recommend seeking out people who have successfully made the change that you are contemplating and ask them what good came of it.

- The chapter, "Why Our Ears and Tongues Do Not Always Work: Communication Part 1" outlines the Whys, or the reasons people do not listen, reasons they do not communicate, and reasons they do not listen deeply or empathize. It becomes clear that we are born with the desire and equipment to communicate. If we truly understand the whys causing us not to listen well, not to speak well and/or not to listen at all, the next chapter's *Rules Of Engagement* are fairly straightforward. We must understand and be willing to reduce the faulty thinking and pathology that act as barriers to good human interconnectedness. If you can be honest enough with yourself, or you have received credible feedback that you have come to accept, to indicate that you are a poor listener or poor communicator, you are halfway home! Having let this information in, you can probably then proceed to review the whys presented in the chapter, select the ones that are your communication stumbling blocks, and begin to turn them into building blocks. The usual rules apply: Get good support, be open to unpleasant news, and be prepared to take small steps one at a time.

- "Rules of Engagement: Communication Part 2" is primarily a how-to chapter. It begins, however, with the idea that having explored the overall picture of why people do not listen and communicate well, we can apply honest, in-depth cost-benefit analysis in exploring particularly why Me, Inc does not communicate well. What follows then is a quite detailed "manual" which trains you in how to engage in empathic listening and how to communicate clearly and assertively.

    In self-examining why you are having listening and/or communication problems, if you find yourself resorting to the old blame game of putting the reasons on other people in your present environment or on your "dysfunctional family," *stop!* The blame will not move you forward, and will probably even set you back and delay your growth. By blaming, you are distancing yourself from the issue and failing to own it.

- The idea behind the next chapter, "Create Unsinkable Relation-*Ships*: Value Propositions Of Relationships," is that just as we should take into account not only the cost, but also the long-term value, of purchasing something or making a business deal, we should also subject our human relationships to such scrutiny. At one point, I state emphatically that, *"We only stay actively involved in relationships that we are getting something out of."* What doing Value Propositions on relationships involves is rooting out what the good and bad somethings are that we are getting out of a current relationship or that we believe we will get out of a relationship we may enter. They also keep this process mindful and active, rather than on the "hidden agenda" level.

    As with so many of the concepts and techniques discussed in *CLO*, this one requires deep and penetrating self-analysis, and as I said in the chapter, "doing Value Propositions on relationships is not for the faint of heart." Again, as we have so often encountered, it is not wise to go ahead with your Value Propositions without getting the support and input of trusted people in your life. So *even if you are not, but especially if you are* having difficulty doing a deep, honest Value Proposition on one or more of the relationships in your life, seek out and listen openly to your support system. As part of any relationship Value Proposition work, search deeply into what in Chapter 9, Figure 9.2, we call Inner Supports. These are your deepest values and beliefs, your spiritual Higher Powers, and those memories that helped create and still help you maintain your belief systems. In the relationships we choose, perhaps more than in any other area of our lives, it is critical to remain true to our interpersonal styles, our likes and dislikes, and most importantly our deeply held convictions.

A second common challenge that people have in applying Value Propositions to relationships is that the whole idea may seem repulsive. "Relationships are about love, caring, those invisible, magical bonds that tie people together," you may be objecting. "What are you doing applying this business concept to something so sacred?" Problem relationships are *very often* rooted at least partly in the participants' refusal or inability to apply such tough-minded ideas as Value Propositions in their choices of people and how to relate to those people. I believe this process that some would refer to as "cold" is actually in the end what creates very warm and loving relationships.

- Finally, in "CEO Roundtables and Masterminds: Support Systems For The You Business," I discuss the critical importance of not "going it alone," either in business or in personal life. I describe the various types of support, the need for an adequate quality and quantity of people to fill the various positions on the support team, and the need for "backup" in the form of core beliefs, plus memories and other means of grounding us in those beliefs. We need to not only have available but also access our support systems, and the functioning of the support systems must ultimately be aimed at problem-solving, not just criticism, complaining or venting.

You may find that you are frequently going to the wrong people for support, or that you are failing to access your support system. You may also discover that your support system offers nothing more than commiserating, criticizing and complaining, or that you are using it for nothing more than these purposes. If so, then you need to confront these issues. Do a cost-benefit analysis and a deep search for what the payoffs are to your own commiserating, criticizing and complaining, and be ready to use assertive communication to ask the members of your support system to behave differently. Consider the possibility of having to "fire" some of the members of your support system and find others to replace them.

This chapter also outlines good problem-solving processes. While problem-solving is dependent to a large degree on the support systems, it also involves common sense, good observation, good communication and open-mindedness. When a problem is causing anxiety, or is difficult to solve, or there is outside pressure to solve it, caution needs to be taken to avoid just throwing any solution at the problem to relieve these pressures.

- Remember that above all else, the people in our lives are the greatest assets. So, when you are done reading, go find a big round table with plenty of advisors at it and get to work on Me, Inc.

Keep in mind that Your Life Is The Most Important Business You Will Ever Own. If you have questions or need more information, contact me at: Amy Remmele, Peak Of Success, 331 Alberta Drive, Amherst, New York 14226, 716-626-5977 or go to my website www. peakofsuccess.com.

References

Bath, Kent and Remmele, Amy. *Empathy and Communication Training Manual and DVD*. Buffalo, NY: Pogo Publications, 2004.

Buckingham, Marcus and Clifton, Donald. *Now Discover Your Strengths*. New York: The Free Press, 2001.

Chapin, Harry. *Cat's In the Cradle* (song), 1974.

Chapin, Henry Dwight. "Family vs. Institution," *Survey, 55* (January 15, 1926), 485-488.

Collins, Jim. *Good To Great*. New York: HarperCollins Publishers, 2001.

Covey, Stephen. *The Seven Habits of Highly Effective People*. New York: Fireside, 1989.

De Becker, Gavin. *Protecting the Gift*. New York: The Dial Press, 1999.

De Becker, Gavin. *The Gift of Fear*. New York: Dell, 1999.

Deep, Sam and Sussman, Lyle. *Close the Deal: 120 Checklists for Sales Success*. Cambridge, MA: Basic Books, 1998.

Gladwell, Malcolm. *Blink: The Power of Thinking Without Thinking*. Boston: Back Bay Books, 2007.

Gottman, John. *The Seven Principles for Making Marriage Work*. New York: Three Rivers Press, 1999.

Hanh, Thich Nhat. *Breathe, You Are Alive*. Berkeley, CA: Parallax Press, 1996.

Inscape Publishing Company. 6465 Wayzata Boulevard, Suite 800, Minneapolis, MN 55426, www.inscapepublishing.com.

Kabat-Zinn, Jon. *Wherever You Go, There You Are*. New York: Hyperion, 2005.

Kundtz, David. *Stopping*. Berkeley, CA: Conari Press, 1998.

Maslow, Abraham. "A Theory of Human Motivation," *Psychological Review, 50* (4) (1943), 370 –396.

McGibbon, Josann and Parriott, Sara. *Runaway Bride* (film), 1999.

Oliansky, Joel and Sackheim, William. *The Competition* (film), 1980.

Prochaska, James, Norcross, John and DiClemente, Carlo. *Changing for Good*. New York: Avon Books, 1994.

Salter Ainsworth, Mary D, Blehar, Mary C., Waters, Everett and Wall, Sally. *Patterns of Attachment: A Psychological Study of the Strange Situation*. Hillsdale, NJ: Lawrence Erlbaum, 1979.

Sandler, David. *You Can't Teach a Kid To Ride a Bike At a Seminar: The Sandler Sales Institute's 7-Step System for Successful Selling*. New York: E.P. Dutton, 2000.

Schofield, William. *Psychotherapy: The Purchase of Friendship*. Englewood Cliffs, NJ: Prentice-Hall, 1964.

Shoda, Yuichi, Mischel, Walter and Peake, Phillip. "Predicting Adolescent Cognitive and Self-regulatory Competencies from Preschool Delay of Gratification," *Developmental Psychology, 26* (6) (1990), 978-986.

Stone, Oliver and Weiser, Stanley. *Wall Street* (film), 1987.

TIPS (Topics In Patient Safety), The Newsletter of the VA National Center for Patient Safety, *4*, 5 (November/December, 2004), http://www.patientsafety.gov/mtt/.

Truax, Charles and Carkhuff, Robert. *Toward Effective Counseling and Psychotherapy: Training and Practice.* Chicago: Aldine Publishing, 1969.

About The Author

Amy Remmele is the owner of Peak of Success, a coaching and consulting business. In her practice with individuals, Amy specializes in working with women who are in difficult or challenging relationships, with professional women who want to stand out and make a mark, and with couples. Amy also consults with businesses, creating synergy by helping each individual to be the best *Chief Life Officer* they can be so that the whole becomes greater than the sum of its parts. Amy speaks to audiences who want to manage their lives and businesses effectively and who want to create unsinkable relation-*ships*.

Amy has been married to her business partner, Dr. Kent Bath, for over 30 years. They are the parents of an eighteen-year-old daughter and thirteen-year-old twin sons. Working and living together have afforded Kent and Amy the privilege of teaching their children sound psychological guidelines and business principles. As a result, Amy has been fortunate enough to be able to "field test" her *Chief Life Officer* lessons in a fun and safe environment, with cooperative and willing participants.

Amy and Kent are the co-authors of their book, ***Re-Phrase It: Adding Empathy and Emotional Intelligence to Your Everyday Life***, and of their relationship workbook, ***Empathy, Communication and Conflict Resolution Home Study Program***, and co-producers of the six-hour self-help video, ***Life Enhancement***. Amy also writes a monthly column for the ***After 50 News***.

CLO Bonus!

Hear

The Plain White Rapper

Perform
All of the
CLO Chapter Raps!

Download Your Free
MP3 File
at
www.ChiefLifeOfficer.net

BUY A SHARE OF THE FUTURE IN YOUR COMMUNITY

These certificates make great holiday, graduation and birthday gifts that can be personalized with the recipient's name. The cost of one S.H.A.R.E. or one square foot is $54.17. The personalized certificate is suitable for framing and will state the number of shares purchased and the amount of each share, as well as the recipient's name. The home that you participate in "building" will last for many years and will continue to grow in value.

Here is a sample SHARE certificate:

YES, I WOULD LIKE TO HELP!

I support the work that Habitat for Humanity does and I want to be part of the excitement! As a donor, I will receive periodic updates on your construction activities but, more importantly, I know my gift will help a family in our community realize the dream of homeownership. **I would like to SHARE in your efforts against substandard housing in my community!** *(Please print below)*

PLEASE SEND ME _____ SHARES at $54.17 EACH = $ $_____

In Honor Of: _____

Occasion: (Circle One)   HOLIDAY   BIRTHDAY   ANNIVERSARY

    OTHER: _____

Address of Recipient: _____

Gift From: _____ *Donor Address:* _____

Donor Email: _____

I AM ENCLOSING A CHECK FOR $ $_____ PAYABLE TO HABITAT FOR HUMANITY OR PLEASE CHARGE MY VISA OR MASTERCARD *(CIRCLE ONE)*

Card Number _____ Expiration Date: _____

Name as it appears on Credit Card _____ Charge Amount $ _____

Signature _____

Billing Address _____

Telephone # Day _____ Eve _____

PLEASE NOTE: Your contribution is tax-deductible to the fullest extent allowed by law.
Habitat for Humanity • P.O. Box 1443 • Newport News, VA 23601 • 757-596-5553
www.HelpHabitatforHumanity.org

Printed in the USA
CPSIA information can be obtained
at www.ICGtesting.com
JSHW082209140824
68134JS00014B/514